D0906653

The Master Musicians Series

STRAVINSKY

Series edited by
Sir Jack Westrup, MA, HonDMus(Oxon), FRCO
Professor Emeritus of Music, Oxford University

VOLUMES IN THE MASTER MUSICIANS SERIES

Bach *Eva Mary and Sydney Grew*

Bartók *Lajos Lesznai*

Beethoven *Marion M. Scott*

Bellini *Leslie Orrey*

Berlioz *J. H. Elliot*

Brahms *Peter Latham*

Bruckner *Derek Watson*

Chopin *Arthur Hedley*

Debussy *Edward Lockspeiser*

Delius *Alan Jefferson*

Dvořák *Alec Robertson*

Elgar *Ian Parrott*

Franck *Laurence Davies*

Grieg *John Horton*

Handel *Percy M. Young*

Haydn *Rosemary Hughes*

Liszt *Walter Beckett*

Mahler *Michael Kennedy*

Mendelssohn *Philip Radcliffe*

Monteverdi *Denis Arnold*

Mozart *Eric Blom*

Mussorgsky *M. D. Calvocoressi*

Purcell *Sir Jack Westrup*

Schubert *Arthur Hutchings*

Schumann *Joan Chissell*

Sibelius *Robert Layton*

Smetana *John Clapham*

Stravinsky *Francis Routh*

Tchaikovsky *Edward Garden*

Vaughan Williams *James Day*

Verdi *Dyneley Hussey*

Wagner *Robert L. Jacobs*

IN PREPARATION

Berg *Nicholas Chadwick*

Prokofiev *Rita McAllister*

Rakhmaninov *Geoffrey Norris*

Ravel *Roger Nichols*

Schoenberg *Malcolm MacDonald*

Richard Strauss *Michael Kennedy*

Tallis and Byrd *Michael Howard*

THE MASTER MUSICIANS SERIES

STRAVINSKY

by Francis Routh

*With eight pages of plates and
music examples in text*

J. M. DENT & SONS LTD
LONDON

First published 1975
© Text, Francis Routh, 1975

Made in Great Britain
at the
Aldine Press · Letchworth · Herts
for
J. M. DENT & SONS LTD
Aldine House · Albemarle Street · London

This book is set in 11 on 12 point Fournier 185

Hardback ISBN: 0 460 03138 4
Paperback ISBN: 0 460 02171 0

Preface

Stravinsky is the most representative of contemporary composers. His career began at a time when, in the wake of Wagner, Western music had forsaken a single, common language. The period between the wars witnessed a polarization, mainly between the Austro-German school on the one hand, and the Franco-Russian school on the other—of whom the most prominent was Stravinsky. The final period of his life witnessed his bringing together these two streams, so long divided. In this sense his work may be seen as re-uniting and re-vitalizing twentieth-century music.

Few composers have been better and more fully documented. Not only has he himself written extensively about his own work, but numerous writers, ranging from Ramuz to Craft, have already given valuable first-hand accounts of his life and music. But the definitive biography must await the study of the large amount of material that is just beginning to appear in the USSR, as well as of other papers. Meanwhile this book takes the facts as known at present.

I have referred to the stage works by their French titles in the text; thus *Le Rossignol*, not *The Nightingale*. Occasional ambiguities in titles, however, remain to haunt the conscientious editor. For instance, the *Octet* is published, and generally known, under that title; yet Stravinsky referred to 'my *Octuor*'. So which is one to use? Until a more durable solution presents itself, in this imperfect world, I have elected to use both, in different contexts.

Quotation marks in the text indicate that a particular word or phrase is being quoted *verbatim* from one of Stravinsky's own writings.

The identification of a passage in a score is by means of the customary figures. The plus sign indicates bars following; the minus sign indicates bars preceding. Thus for example:

(page 99) fig. 170—2 indicates two bars before figure 170.
(page 120) fig. 10+1 indicates one bar after figure 10.
(page 95, Music Ex. 3) $\boxed{55}$+1 indicates one bar after figure 55.

The chart given as Example 24 (pages 138–9) shows the series in their original forms only. Each series has four possible forms: O(riginal), I(nversion), R(etrograde) and R(etrograde) I(nversion). The other three may easily be worked from the original version.

I acknowledge with gratitude the generous help of William Bardwell, Robert Craft, Dr Hans Heimler, Theodore Stravinsky, and Eric Walter White, who read the text and gave many useful suggestions; also of Mrs Vanessa Cunningham, who prepared the typescript. My particular thanks are due to Miss Janet Osborn of CBS Records for generously supplying records, photographs and other valuable material; also to Miss Sally Cavender of Boosey & Hawkes for her painstaking assistance with many aspects of the book.

Of the music examples, Nos. 1, 8, 9, 11, 14–19, 21–23a, 25 and 26 are reproduced by permission of the copyright owners Boosey & Hawkes Music Publishers Ltd; No. 12 is reproduced by permission of J. & W. Chester/Edition Wilhelm Hansen London Ltd; Nos. 3–7, 10, 13, 20 and 23b are the copyright of B. Schott's Söhne and are reproduced by permission of Schott & Co. Ltd; the series shown in No. 24 are my copyright.

London, 1974   Francis Routh

Contents

THE LIFE

PREFACE — v

1 Childhood, adolescence, preparation — 1
2 Fulfilment and scandal — 6
3 From *Le Rossignol* to *Pulcinella* — 14
4 The last of the Russian works — 25
5 A new classicism — 30
6 A fresh start — 43
7 American citizen — 50
8 Final fulfilment — 58
9 Envoi — 64
  Interlude — 70

THE MUSIC

10 Stage works (I) — 72
11 Stage works (II) — 83
12 Orchestral works — 92
13 Works for solo instruments. Concertos — 102
14 Ensemble and chamber music. Songs for solo voice — 111
15 Cantatas and choral works — 118
16 Stravinsky's music: style and idea — 130
17 Stravinsky's aesthetic — 146

APPENDICES

A Calendar   153
B Catalogue of works   168
C Personalia   179
D Bibliography   188
E Notes on the Stravinsky family   192
  INDEX   193

Illustrations

BETWEEN PAGES 86 AND 87

Stravinsky with his four children. Clarens, 1915 (*Archives Theodore Stravinsky*)

In Hollywood, 1944 (*Boosey & Hawkes Music Publishers Ltd*)

Claudio Arrau (*L*) and Joseph Szigeti (*R*). New York, 1946 (*Boosey & Hawkes Music Publishers Ltd*)

With Robert Craft (*R*) and Franco Autori (*L*). New York, 1953 (*Columbia Records, U.S.A., courtesy of Boosey & Hawkes Ltd*)

With George Balanchine, rehearsing *Agon*, 1957 (*Boosey & Hawkes Music Publishers Ltd*)

At a recording session, 1960 (*CBS Records*)

In Hollywood, 1964 (*CBS Records*)

With Derrik Olsen and Lina Lalandi, after conducting *Oedipus Rex*. Athens, 1966 (*CBS Records*)

1 Childhood, adolescence, preparation

The name 'Stravinsky' comes from 'Strava', a small river in eastern Poland; and the family name was originally Soulima-Stravinsky, though when the territory changed to Russia, in the reign of Catherine the Great, the prefix was removed.

Igor Fedorovich Stravinsky was born, according to the modern calendar, on 18th June 1882, at Oranienbaum, on the Gulf of Finland, some thirty miles west of St Petersburg, now Leningrad. He had three brothers: Roman (1874–95), Youry (1879–1941) and Goury (1884–1917). His mother was Anna Kholodovsky, whose father Kiril lived in Kiev and was a minister of agriculture under the Tsar. His father Feodor Ignatievich, who had a law degree at Kiev, was a bass singer, first at the Kiev opera, later at the opera in St Petersburg—one of the focal points of Russian music at this time.

Igor's father, though a man of wide culture, was subject to sudden, uncontrollable bouts of temper; their relationship was therefore a distant one, only becoming closer when the child, whose health was delicate, became ill. Of his brothers, Goury alone excited his real affection. Roman studied law until his early death in 1895; Youry became an architectural engineer, living in St Petersburg until his death. But Goury, like Igor, also studied law, until he decided to pursue singing professionally. He had a baritone voice, and the *Two Poems of Verlaine* (1910) were later written for him. The two brothers were constant companions, and Goury's death in 1917, while serving on the Roumanian front, was a deep blow to the composer.

As a child Igor read omnivorously: Tolstoy, Shakespeare, Dante and translations from the Greek. He was particularly excited by Sophocles' *Oedipus Rex*. His father possessed a large and famous library, with first editions of Gogol, Pushkin and Tolstoy, as well as operatic scores. In music it was as a pianist that his parents had aspirations for him, and at the age of nine he was taught the piano, first by Mlle Snetkova, daughter of a musician in the Maryinsky Theatre orchestra, later by Mlle Kashperova, a pupil of Anton Rubinstein. He came to know the works of Wagner and Rimsky-Korsakov from the piano scores; but generally speaking his adolescence was a period of mounting frustration and bitterness. He was gradually approaching the moment when his individualism would break loose and his nascent creativity first assert itself.

During the summer months of each year most middle-class Russian families would leave the city for the country. The Stravinsky family were no exception, and between 1896 and 1900 Igor and his brother Goury spent the summer at the remote Volhynian village of Oustilug, about 100 miles south of Brest-Litovsk. This was a small Jewish community at the confluence of the Louga and the Bug, some two and a half days' journey from St Petersburg; and it was here that Gabriel Nossenko, married to their mother's sister Maria, had bought land for his daughters Ludmilla and Catherine. Catherine ('Katia') had been a childhood friend to Igor ever since their first meeting in 1891. Common interests drew them together—painting and amateur theatricals, as well as piano playing—and after she had studied singing in Paris she was a source of great encouragement to him.

Although they were first cousins, they were married on 24th January 1906. They built a new house on the Nossenko estate at Oustilug, by the river, which proved to be a 'haven for composing' until 1914, when the war cut them off from Russia altogether. The song-suite *The Faun and the Shepherdess* was written in the year of their marriage, partly indeed while on honeymoon in Finland, and was naturally dedicated to Catherine.

From his sixteenth year onwards the young Stravinsky constantly attended opera performances at the Maryinsky Theatre, where his father occupied a prominent position. It was thus in the theatre, with the strong, endemic tradition of Russian opera it represented, that his creative personality was first formed. He saw *The Sleeping Beauty* when he was 'seven or eight'; Glinka's *Life for the Tsar* was another early childhood experience, as well as that composer's *Russlan and Ludmilla*, in which his father sang the role of Farlaf. His father was particularly noted for his performance in *Lohengrin*; also the drunken scene in *Prince Igor*, on which Rimsky-Korsakov modelled a similar scene in his *Sadko*, of which the young Stravinsky witnessed the first production. But all the Russian composers of this time—Glinka, Dargomijsky, Serov; Liadov, Belaiev, Glazunov, Tcherepnin, Scriabin, Arensky; Cui, Mussorgsky, Borodin, Balakirev, Rimsky-Korsakov (the group known as 'The Five'); and, supremely, Tchaikovsky—excited his deep curiosity.

He met the intelligentsia of St Petersburg, poets and artists as well as composers, and was made aware of achievements in other artistic fields than music. He saw the great plays of Chekhov and other Russian dramatists in the company of his close friend Stepan Mitusov, who in due course (1908) helped to provide him with the libretto of his own first opera, *Le Rossignol*.

He attended St Petersburg University for four years, 1901–1905, allegedly studying criminal law and legal philosophy, but his time was chiefly filled with music; and following his father's death in 1902 he was better able to follow his natural bent. Earlier that year he had first been introduced to Rimsky-Korsakov, who encouraged him to pursue music lessons. Accordingly he studied with him, but privately, not at the Conservatoire; and over the next six years, until the elder composer's death in 1908, an extremely close relationship developed between the

3

two. In form and orchestration Rimsky's approach was strict, patient; but Stravinsky found his teacher on the whole uninterested in new music from France or Germany. On the other hand, he provided not only the advice, criticism and encouragement of a master to his pupil, but also something of a father's care and affection.

In addition to the performances of opera, Stravinsky's interest and musical awareness were further stimulated by the wider concert-life of St Petersburg. He found the programmes of the Imperial Symphony Orchestra on the whole dull and unenterprising, while Belaiev's concerts promoted chiefly 'The Five'. His own first orchestral success was to be due to the conductor Alexander Siloti; but it was at one of the 'Evenings of Contemporary Music' that he first had an opportunity to hear some of his own compositions, when Nicolas Richter played his *Piano Sonata in F sharp minor*; he himself accompanied Mlle Petrenko in his Gorodetzsky songs. These 'Evenings of Contemporary Music', though small and informal, made a lasting impression on Stravinsky. Not only did they give a much needed hearing to the works of young Russian composers; they also included music of the newly unfolding French school of Debussy, Ravel, Dukas and d'Indy, as well as early music by Couperin, Monteverdi and Bach.

Rimsky-Korsakov used to hold weekly gatherings at his house, when his pupils' compositions were played; and these occasions were another valuable experience to the apprentice composer. On 6th March 1903 he played his *Plaisanteries Musicales*; while a year later 'the young Rimsky-Korsakovs, with Stravinsky at their head, performed a charming cantata which Stravinsky had composed'. It is not therefore surprising that Stravinsky's first substantial orchestral piece, the *Symphony in E flat*, should be dedicated to his teacher. Meanwhile a friendship soon sprang up between him and Rimsky's two sons, Andrei and Vladimir, who played the cello and violin respectively. With the two daughters there was not quite the same closeness, though Nadezhda's voice inspired the *Pastorale*; and when she married the composer Maximilian Steinberg in 1908 Stravinsky wrote his orchestral fantasy *Fireworks* in celebration. It was during these years, and with this particular work, that he first became aware of the artistic dichotomy, and the choice he would soon need to make, between the established, well-tried methods of the Conservatoire musicians, such as Glazunov, on whose model the *Symphony in E flat* was based, and the more hazardous, uncertain path of individualism and self-discovery; between a narrow nationalism, represented by 'The Five', and a wider cosmopolitanism; in a word, between the old and the new.

As it happened, events helped him to choose. The *avant-garde* were grouped around Sergey Diaghilev. This remarkable man, ten years older than Stravinsky but also at St Petersburg University, and also a pupil of Rimsky-Korsakov at the Conservatoire, was far more than just an impresario. He had a thorough knowledge of music, painting, choreography. He was the originator and coordinator of grandiose schemes, with at the same time an unfailing flair for recognizing, and sparking off, the potentiality of success. Over the coming years he was destined to synthesize the *Ballets Russes*, and to build this unique company as much on the décor of Benois, Bakst, Roerich, Picasso, and on the choreography of Fokine, Massine, Nijinska, Balanchine, as on the music of numerous composers—pre-eminently his young fellow countryman, Stravinsky.

In the early years of the twentieth century, before Diaghilev changed its course, Russian ballet tended to be conventionalized, formal, and had then less prestige than the opera. It seemed unbelievable that it was to be through the ballet that a great new modern movement was about to be born. The catalyst was Diaghilev, and his young choreographer, Mikhail Fokine.

2   Fulfilment and scandal

That Diaghilev should have embarked on the creation of his *Ballets Russes* at the precise moment when Stravinsky was just reaching his first moments of individual identity as a composer, is one of those extraordinary historical coincidences for which neither satisfactory reason nor convincing explanation is possible. It happened; we must leave it at that. However tempting it may be to speculate about what Diaghilev's work would have been without Stravinsky, or to what end Stravinsky's early work would have been directed without Diaghilev, such questions are unanswerable. According to one eye-witness, Pierre Souvtchinsky, Diaghilev did not 'discover' Stravinsky; rather Stravinsky 'happened' to him. Each, moreover, needed the other.

It was through Diaghilev that, at the early age of twenty-eight, Stravinsky first achieved real success and international acclaim; it was through Stravinsky that Diaghilev, in the period of twenty years until his death in 1929, made his *Ballets Russes* not merely a focus of creative energy, but a musical force to be reckoned with; and not merely among already converted balleto-manes, but among a much wider and cosmopolitan circle of contemporary musicians.

Diaghilev, whose theatrical activities began in 1906, with *Boris Godunov*, heard two works of Stravinsky at an orchestral concert in St Petersburg in February 1909, conducted by Alexander Siloti: the *Scherzo Fantastique* and *Fireworks*. After this he invited the young composer, among others, to orchestrate some of Chopin's music for a production of *Les Sylphides* later that year in Paris. As it happened, Diaghilev's Paris season in 1909 was a sensation, chiefly thanks to the production of Rimsky-Korsakov's *Sheherazade*, with sumptuous décor and costumes by Léon Bakst.

In turning to Stravinsky as the composer for *The Firebird*, which was planned for his Paris production the next season, 1910, Diaghilev proved his shrewd judgment as well as his flair for novelty and freshness. There were several other possible composers whom he might have chosen: Tcherepnin or Liadov, for instance. Indeed, Benois and Tcherepnin collaborated in *Pavillon d'Armide* that very year. But perhaps Diaghilev had heard of Stravinsky's strong predilection for the theatre; perhaps he even heard of his newly begun fairy-tale opera *Le Rossignol*. *The Firebird* was also a fairy tale, based on old Russian legends.

But both the story and the commission made the twenty-seven-year-old Stravinsky hesitate—or so he says. Would he be required to write merely descriptive music? Were Diaghilev and his company looking for another Rimsky-Korsakov? Would he be able to finish the score in six months? Moreover his opera would have to be laid on one side. It took the combined diplomacy of Diaghilev, Fokine, Bakst, Nijinsky and Benois to dispel his doubts—if indeed he ever really had any.

The score of *The Firebird*, dedicated to Rimsky-Korsakov, is a brilliant study in orchestral effects. The libretto was by Fokine, though others, particularly Bakst, also contributed to the scenario. From this first experience in the theatre Stravinsky learnt much, especially from Fokine, whose requirements were precise and exact, in spite of his insistence that the music was simply an accompaniment to the dance. In later years, when their relationship soured, Fokine would refer to *The Firebird* as Stravinsky's musical accompaniment to *his* 'choreographic poem'.

At the 1910 performance Stravinsky's ideas for the dancers were not fully realized; but his protests were ineffectual. Even the conductor of the orchestra, Gabriel Pierné, took him publicly to task for one of his markings in the score. As with many a young composer, on his first important professional appearance, Stravinsky was made to learn the hard way. Moreover his notoriety was envied and resented by his St Petersburg colleagues, and their estrangement was to prove permanent.

On the credit side, he had been introduced for the first time to an international audience. Among the many celebrities at the glittering first night at the Paris Opéra were Debussy and Ravel. In the same year there was a production of Debussy's *Pelléas et Mélisande*, which Stravinsky saw, and which, despite his later protestations of boredom, was to influence him greatly. The success of *The Firebird* was total, unqualified; it has remained so ever since. Immediately after the première he made an orchestral suite of the ballet score, taking those sections that seemed best to him.

That same year, although *Le Rossignol* still awaited completion, following the success of *The Firebird*, Stravinsky embarked on two new large-scale works, the ideas of which already existed in his mind. The first idea of *Le Sacre du printemps* had come to him as he was just finishing *The Firebird* in St Petersburg, in the spring of 1910. It was a vision of a pagan rite, with elders seated in a circle, watching a young girl dance herself to death as a sacrifice to propitiate the god of spring. Stravinsky described this to his friend the painter Nicolas Roerich, who was well versed in Russian folklore and legend; later also to Diaghilev. The seeds of *Le Sacre* had been sown.

But, like *The Firebird*, the theme of *Le Sacre* was concerned with an unreal world of fantasy, and meanwhile Stravinsky wished to 'refresh' himself with an orchestral piece in which the piano would be prominent. He had in mind a puppet, exasperating the orchestra

with diabolical cascades of *arpeggi*. The orchestra in turn retaliates with menacing trumpet-blasts. The outcome is a terrific noise which

8

reaches its climax and ends in the sorrowful and querulous collapse of the poor puppet. Having finished this bizarre piece, I struggled for hours, while walking beside Lake Geneva, to find a title which would express in a word the character of my music and consequently the personality of this creature.

Soon he found it: *Petrushka*, the immortal and unhappy hero of the fairground, common to all countries, whether as Guignol or Punch.

It did not take long for him to be persuaded by Diaghilev of the balletic possibilities of such a theme, and together they discussed the action. It would take place at the Shrovetide Fair in St Petersburg; there would be three characters; Benois would be entrusted with the scenario, Fokine with the choreography. When the ballet was first presented in Paris at the Théâtre du Châtelet on 13th June 1911, it too began a success that has continued ever since. It has exercised a unique hold on the public. Whatever reservations Stravinsky had about Fokine's staging, he had none at all about Vaslav Nijinsky's dancing of the title-role, or Tamara Karsavina as the ballerina. As a whole the work unmistakably possessed that brilliant fusion of opposites that ensured its success on the stage, then and now: the pathos of Petrushka set against the glitter of the fair; the world of imagination set against the world of reality; the use of traditional folksong set against Stravinsky's own style.

No special version was needed for concert-hall use; the ballet-score was used as it stood. When, some years later, in 1921, Stravinsky made a virtuoso three-movement piano suite of *Petrushka* for Artur Rubinstein, it was not so much a transcription as 'an act of restitution' to its original conception, as a piano-centred *Konzertstück*. From *Petrushka* stems another important development—Stravinsky's association with Sergey Koussevitzky, who from now on published his music in his Édition Russe.

After the Paris season Stravinsky returned to Oustilug.

Already ideas for *Le Sacre du printemps* were forming in his mind which he was anxious to discuss with Roerich. The two met in July at Talachkino, the estate near Smolensk belonging to the Princess Tenichev, a noted patron of Russian art, with a considerable collection of her own. The visual and scenic details, and the sequence of episodes, were settled in a few days; Roerich also sketched some of the décor, and designed costumes modelled on those in the Princess's collection. Stravinsky made a start on the score as soon as he returned to Oustilug; but it was at Clarens in Switzerland, where he went with his family in the autumn, that most of the work was written. The score was finished by late spring, 1912.

Having concentrated his attention on to this score, it was disappointing to be told by Diaghilev that it could not be produced in 1912. The reason had to do with a European tour that Diaghilev had arranged for the company; also with Nijinsky's debut as a choreographer that year. But if Diaghilev imagined that Nijinsky's pre-eminence as a dancer would be equalled by his ability as a choreographer, he can hardly have been prepared for the scandal that ensued after his protégé's first production, *L'Après-midi d'un faune*, to Debussy's music, in which the representation of sexual love, and blatantly erotic gestures, outraged the audience.

Although this only concerned Stravinsky indirectly at the time, it was to have a very direct effect on the production of *Le Sacre du printemps*, which was eventually arranged for 29th May the following year, 1913, to inaugurate the new Théâtre des Champs-Élysées. In spite of his inadequacy for the task, Nijinsky was given the choreography. Even after several months of rehearsals for the dancers, who quickly grasped what was required, Stravinsky had to provide the most elementary musical instruction to the choreographer.

'I will count to forty while you play,' Nijinsky would say to the composer, 'and we will see where we come out.' It was indeed doubly unfortunate that a choreographer who was ignorant of even the barest rudiments of music should have been assigned the task of directing the dancing for a score which, in the event, was to prove a highly complex rhythmical treasure-chest and, moreover, one that has challenged and intrigued musicians from that day to this. The orchestra was in the capable hands of Pierre Monteux, who had already conducted *Petrushka* in 1911, and sixteen rehearsals had given the orchestral musicians some security.

The scandal at the first performance is now itself part of our twentieth-century folklore. Anecdotes abound, whether true or false, which vary according to the sources. The uproar seems to have been caused just as much by the dancing as by the strangeness of the music. Protests began from the beginning of the performance, starting from the cheap seats in the gallery, and gradually spreading through the house, until they increased to a storm of fury at the *Danse des adolescents*. For this scene Stravinsky had imagined a row of almost motionless dancers; now they jumped grotesquely, with what Cocteau called 'automaton-like monotony'. Was this to be a repetition of Nijinsky's sexual exhibitionism of the previous year? Murmuring gave way to screeching and yelling; demonstration to counter-demonstration.

Florent Schmitt, whose *Tragédie de Salomé* two years earlier was dedicated to 'his friend Igor Stravinsky', shrieked out at the audience: 'Taisez-vous, les grues du Seizième'—referring to the ladies of the elegant sixteenth *arrondissement*. Insults and uninhibited repartee flew back and forth amid the hubbub, which soon degenerated to physical violence. About fifty combatants stripped naked, and were taken into police custody. Those present in the audience became divided into two warring camps —pro-Stravinsky and anti-Stravinsky; many who were not present clearly wished they had been. An outraged Countess was heard to declare, superbly: 'J'ai soixante ans, mais c'est la première fois qu'on a osé se moquer de moi!'

After a few minutes an irate Stravinsky left his seat in the theatre and went backstage, where he found Nijinsky standing on a chair, shouting numbers to the dancers, who could not hear the orchestra through the din. Diaghilev told the electrician to turn the lights off and on. Through all this, Monteux, calm and magisterial, somehow managed to steer the performance to its conclusion, though the noise from the auditorium greatly exceeded the sounds made by his players.

For Stravinsky music was autonomous; nothing could impede that autonomy. *Le Sacre* was the most blatant assertion of that autonomy. So far from ballet music being an accompaniment to the dance, as Fokine had maintained, much to the composer's chagrin, the very reverse held for Stravinsky. For him the music was what mattered, first, last and all the time. He desired, as he says explicitly in his *Chronicles*, that the choreography should express 'a plastic realization, flowing simply and naturally from what the music demanded'. For Stravinsky it was the music which made demands of the choreography, not *vice versa*. The dance makes explicit what is already implicit in the score. The failure of the first production of *Le Sacre* was, therefore, according to the composer, due to Nijinsky's failure to meet the requirements of the music in his dance-movements.

The Nijinsky-Roerich version was seen twice more in Paris, without the attendant scandal of the first night. It was also given three performances in London in July, before being withdrawn.

On 5th April 1914, a year after the notorious première, a concert performance of *Le Sacre* was given in Paris, again with Monteux conducting. This time the chiefly young audience amply made up for the earlier débâcle, and Stravinsky was carried shoulder-high through the streets. The score had begun its world-life as a concert piece; and in spite of several fresh choreographic ideas, starting with a production by Massine in 1920, it was as a concert-work that the composer thereafter preferred it.

Stravinsky had by this time, and hardly surprisingly, become a central figure in Parisian *salons*. Every May the talk of the intelligentsia, to say nothing of its gossip- and rumour-mongers, would centre round the new Stravinsky work which Diaghilev was expected to present. Stravinsky was accepted, indeed welcomed, by the French artistic and intellectual élite; not only by Debussy and Ravel, but by Manuel da Falla, Maurice Delage, Jean Cocteau, Florent Schmitt, and that remarkable American lady, and prominent patron of the *avant-garde*, the Princess Edmond de Polignac. He had, in short, arrived.

3   From *Le Rossignol* to *Pulcinella*

A few days after the first performance of *Le Sacre* Stravinsky fell ill with typhoid fever, and spent six weeks in a nursing home in Neuilly. This prevented his seeing the production of *Khovan-shchina*, which he and Ravel had jointly revised early in 1913 at Diaghilev's request; it also kept him from accompanying Diaghilev to London, where *Le Sacre* was given three further performances at Drury Lane in July. He returned to Oustilug to convalesce. After the severe strain of events in Paris he needed leisure and relaxation; so he took some little improvised melodies, called *Souvenirs de mon enfance*, that he had first played to Rimsky-Korsakov in 1906, and decided to give them the fresh form of songs for voice and piano. These he dedicated to his own three children: Theodore, aged six, *The Jackdaw*; Ludmilla ('Mika'), aged five, *The Rook*; and Soulima, aged three, *The Magpie*. His youngest daughter, Maria Milena, was not born until the following year, 1914.

The songs used popular Russian texts, and the words of the third are pure onomatopœic nonsense; but from this apparently slight source two large stage works were shortly to spring; and over the next few years he was to write several more such light-hearted songs, many centred round the animal world. Indeed, his last original composition (1966) was to be a song of this nature, for his second wife, Vera.[1]

On moving to Clarens for the winter of 1913–14, he received

[1] See p. 66.

a request from the newly founded Théâtre Libre of Moscow for nothing less than the completion of his opera, *Le Rossignol*. This he had begun in 1908, with the active encouragement of Rimsky-Korsakov, who expressed approval of the preliminary sketches. The story by Hans Andersen was a Chinese fantasy, and represented a realistic fairy-tale world, whose lost beauty Stravinsky tried to rediscover several times in later life. Its theme was typically Franco-Russian of the nineteenth century; an interest in things Oriental was something that was felt equally in Paris and St Petersburg at this time. *The Fairy's Kiss* was to be another such attempt.

Since 1909, when he and Mitusov planned it together, *Le Rossignol* had been laid aside with only one act completed, while other major works intervened. In the meantime his style had evolved. Nevertheless Stravinsky decided to make this opera his next major work. He met Mitusov in Warsaw to discuss the libretto, and worked at the score that winter in Switzerland. As it happened, the Moscow theatre did not materialize; but this may well have been a blessing in disguise, as Diaghilev was able to produce it in Paris that summer, with costumes and sets by Benois, and choreography by Boris Romanov. Monteux again conducted, when André Messager declined. The composer later considered this opera to be scenically the most beautiful of his early works with Diaghilev. His concern that the music of Act I would sound less mature than the rest, because it was written four years earlier, and was somewhat 'self-consciously Debussy-ish and Rimsky-ish', proved groundless. But later, in 1917, when he came to arrange the symphonic poem *Chant du Rossignol*, he used only Acts II and III, and even made substantial cuts in them. The opera marked a climax, though not one of Stravinsky's making. After Paris, Diaghilev's company had completed the season in London, but then, almost immediately, war was declared in Europe.

Just before, in July 1914, Stravinsky made what was to prove his last visit to Oustilug. He went to collect folk-poems from there, Warsaw and Kiev, with a view to the libretto of a projected *divertissement* depicting a Russian peasant wedding. He found this material only in the nick of time; it was almost as if he had a premonition of impending events.

During the war he lived in Switzerland, at Morges. His only journeys were to meet Diaghilev and his company, now of necessity largely disbanded. At the age of thirty-two, he found himself cut off from his house at Oustilug, and from all but a slender part of his possessions in Russia; but he was in the company of several artists and musicians, whose new friendship was to prove both lasting and precious: the writer Ramuz, the conductor Ernest Ansermet, the painter René Auberjonois, and Alexandre and Charles-Albert Cingria. Indeed, the war had made Switzerland something of an international meeting-place for artists and musicians from many countries; Busoni, who lived at Zürich, was one, though he and Stravinsky did not meet until 1923 in Weimar.

Stravinsky's sadness at his remoteness from Russia was alleviated by his acquaintance with its folk-poems. It was not so much the meaning of the words, which was often crude, as their sound and cadence, which appealed to his ear. Several small vocal pieces were written to these texts, though the music is original, not folksong: *Pribaoutki*, or 'word-games', for male voice and small orchestra; *Berceuses du chat*, for voice and three clarinets; *Trois histoires pour enfants*, for voice and piano, and *Four Russian peasant songs* ('saucers'), for female choir.

Two larger-scale stage works, based on the style and content of these Russian texts, were already forming in his mind at this time. Indeed, the basic ideas of the first, *Les Noces*, had occurred to him as early as 1912. The theme of a Russian peasant wedding would be presented as a *divertissement* of the masquerade type, with direct quotations of popular verse, which Stravinsky found in the anthologies by Afanasiev and Kireievsky. The latter was the chief source for the material of *Les Noces*, while Afanasiev's anthology gave rise to *Renard* and, later, *Histoire du soldat*.

But meanwhile the war situation made future plans uncertain. Diaghilev, whose company had dispersed, asked Stravinsky to meet him in Florence in the autumn of 1914. Plans to reassemble the company and tour North America were discussed. It was suggested that Stravinsky's projected *Les Noces* might be produced; Diaghilev also put forward another suggestion, *Liturgie*, which was to be a spectacle based on the Mass. This, however, Stravinsky rejected on both sacred and economic grounds; he disagreed with a religious event being presented dramatically in this way; what was more to the point, no satisfactory fee was mentioned.

By 1st November Diaghilev had signed the contract for the American tour, and proposed another meeting in central Italy, this time in Rome, where he had rented an apartment, and where, as usual, he was the centre of an extensive circle, which included the 'Futurists' and Marinetti. Stravinsky met him there early in February 1915, when the other visitors included Lord Berners and Prokofiev. He took with him, among other works, three light-hearted piano duets, as well as Afanasiev's anthology of Russian poems; and this bore fruit in the work of Prokofiev. He was nine years younger than Stravinsky, and they had met in 1906 in St Petersburg; he was in Rome now, at Diaghilev's invitation, to discuss a ballet. This was his first visit abroad, and he was to play his second Piano Concerto in Rome. He and Stravinsky played *Petrushka* as a duet. When Stravinsky showed him Afanasiev's anthology, he picked out one poem for his first ballet, *The Buffoon*, which Diaghilev commissioned.

On his return to Switzerland, Stravinsky resumed work on *Les Noces*. *Renard* was also started, which continued the word-play of *Pribaoutki*. In the spring Diaghilev moved to Switzerland, and again became the focus of a group of musicians and dancers, including Massine, Bakst and Ansermet. He was re-forming his company in preparation for their forthcoming visit to America, and in December of that year he gave two charity performances in aid of the Red Cross, one in Geneva and the other in Paris. He looked on these performances as a dress-rehearsal for the American tour, and they included two important débuts; first, that of Massine as a choreographer, in *Soleil de Minuit* (taken from Rimsky-Korsakov's *The Snow Maiden*); second, that of Stravinsky himself as a conductor, of the suite *The Firebird*. Diaghilev wanted Stravinsky to accompany him to America, and conduct his own work at the Metropolitan in New York; but the contract did not mention Stravinsky specifically as a conductor, and he declined. Ansermet had, at Stravinsky's suggestion, replaced Monteux and Pierné, when those two left the Russian Ballet in 1914.

The company left for America on New Year's Day, 1916. Stravinsky remained a few days in Paris, and saw Princess Polignac, who suggested to him a private performance at her house, when conditions eased after the war, of a small work using a chamber orchestra of about twenty players. His attention at that time was focused on the two works taken from Russian folk-poems that he was working on. *Les Noces* was being written for Diaghilev; on the other hand *Renard* was still only an embryonic sketch. When he mentioned this, the Princess expressed approval. So immediately on his return to Switzerland Stravinsky laid aside *Les Noces* and concentrated on *Renard*. Ramuz had already worked on the French translation of the little Russian songs; now he was asked to undertake the much larger task of translation of the Russian text of *Renard*, which, as in the case of *Les Noces*, Stravinsky had adapted himself from folk-poems.

In March he received a surprise visit from Nijinsky, with his wife and child. Nijinsky had been interned in Hungary, but had just been released, and was on his way to join Diaghilev and the company in New York. Stravinsky even tried to persuade the dancer to agree to appear in America only if he himself conducted. This request, which came to nothing, was partly due to the extreme shortage of money which he was experiencing at the time.

The company returned at the end of May, and Stravinsky met them in Madrid. It was his first visit to Spain, and he was highly responsive to the ethos of that country. Some of the street-band music made a vivid impression on him, and he used it later in *Histoire du soldat*. Diaghilev was presenting several ballets at the Theatre Royal, including *The Firebird* and *Petrushka*, and the composer was presented to the king and queen.

The remainder of the summer and autumn were spent on *Renard*, and also on some simple piano duets for Theodore and Mika. The pieces recall scenes; the *Galop* is a caricature of the St Petersburg version of the Folies Bergère; the *Española* was written on his return from Spain. The following March saw Stravinsky again in Rome, where Diaghilev was presenting a Russian Ballet season at the Costanzi Theatre. Along with many old friends, Diaghilev's party this time included someone new to Stravinsky, Pablo Picasso. He, with Cocteau, was discussing the production of *Parade*. After Rome the company moved to Naples, where Massine was presenting his second ballet, *The Good-Humoured Ladies*, to the music of Domenico Scarlatti, orchestrated by Tommasini. This performance, and its implications, which greatly impressed Stravinsky, was to have far-reaching effects later. On his return to Switzerland, he added appropriately a *Napolitana* to his set of piano duets. During the remainder of that year he turned his attention again to *Les Noces*, with Ramuz once more the collaborator. This piece, however, together with *Renard*, had to wait for several years after the war before being staged.

The year 1917 marked a low ebb in the fortunes of Stravinsky and his friends. Not only was he deprived of income and properties in Russia, but, in the event, the Russian Revolution of October 1917 kept him from returning. He was never to see Oustilug again, not even during his return visit to Poland in 1965. Moreover Diaghilev's company, after another American tour, were once again faced with disbandment through lack of engagements.

What was to be the composer's next task? The success of his work with Ramuz over *Renard* and *Les Noces* invited a fresh collaboration; but to what end should their energies be directed? The stage presentation of *Renard* and *Les Noces* appeared remote and hardly feasible; yet what was feasible?

Ramuz describes the genesis of *Histoire du soldat* in the spring of 1917:

Why not do something simple? Why not write a piece which dispenses with a large room, and a large public? A piece whose music would only require a small number of instruments, and would only have two or three characters.

As there are no longer any theatres, we would be our own theatre. We would provide our own sets, which would be mounted without trouble anywhere, even in the open air.

So *Histoire du soldat* owed its existence to the stringent exigencies of war time. It was also planned, by the committee of its creators, to take it round the Swiss villages, a *théâtre ambulant*. As far as the scoring for small orchestra is concerned, Stravinsky was continuing in the direction already chosen for *Renard*; moreover the collaborators turned once again to Afanasiev's collection for the story; this time one called 'The Soldier and the Devil'.

Histoire du soldat was conceived as a story to be read, played and danced. The stage with actors would be in the centre, with the musicians on one side and the reader on the other. These three complementary elements would alternate in solos and ensembles. Stravinsky's score was to be independent, capable of separate performance as a concert suite.

The work was finished by the summer of 1918. Stravinsky and Ramuz then set about finding performers, largely among the students of Lausanne University, where Ansermet had once been Professor of Mathematics. The first performance took place on 28th September that year, at the Lausanne Theatre. Ansermet conducted, Auberjonois designed set and costumes; it was a production which satisfied the composer completely. It was also something of an occasion, thanks to the presence of the Grand Duchess Helen, and the considerable colony of Russian aristocracy then living in Ouchy. Unfortunately a single performance only was possible, and any thoughts the organizers had of touring round Switzerland had to be abandoned when, one by one, the participants, including Stravinsky, succumbed to an epidemic of Spanish influenza. Public halls were even closed by law.

Histoire du soldat marks a turning point in Stravinsky's creative life for more than one reason. First, the practical requirements of a small *théâtre ambulant* replace fantasy; instead of the far-off world of Hans Andersen, or pagan Russia, Afanasiev's story is brought up to date, and the soldier appears as a Swiss private of 1918. Indeed, how could Stravinsky and Ramuz be unaware of the world war that was at that very moment changing the face and character of Europe? Second, in this work for the first time Stravinsky admits fresh influences on his work, both technically and aesthetically. Technically, *Histoire du soldat* is a compendium of rhythmical and metrical devices, of the sort that he had developed consistently since *Fireworks* (1908); aesthetically, he admits the outside influence of jazz. The work had a wide vogue in Europe, particularly in schools, in the 1920s.

In 1918, after returning from the second American tour with the Diaghilev company the previous year, Ansermet had brought Stravinsky a bundle of ragtime music in the form of piano reductions and instrumental parts—which Stravinsky eagerly proceeded to copy out in score. With these pieces before him he composed the *Ragtime* in *Histoire de soldat*. Indeed his choice of instruments very nearly made up a ragtime band. He had not yet heard any jazz; he had only seen printed copies. The immediate effect of the American jazz style on Stravinsky's rhythmic technique may be gauged by comparing the March with which *Renard* opens with the Soldier's March in *Histoire du soldat*.

More important, Stravinsky's assimilation of this fresh musical element heralded that process of widening and enlarging his language that was to mark his work progressively from then on. It is also reasonable to conjecture that the comparatively slow-moving pace of the war years in Switzerland, as well as his discussions with Ramuz, Ansermet and others, caused him to re-examine radically and re-assess the aesthetic and technical bases of his work.

Financial backing for *Histoire du soldat* came from Werner Reinhart. As he was a clarinettist, Stravinsky expressed his gratitude by writing three short pieces for him for solo clarinet. Next, following *Histoire du soldat*, he wrote *Ragtime* for eleven instruments. He began it in October 1918, and finished it on 11th November, just at the time of the armistice. He wrote it also as a piano solo, and played it in this form himself. He saw this as the new dance music, of which his music was a composite portrait, just as past composers had written concert pieces round the dances of their day, such as the waltz or the mazurka. Stravinsky never embarked on any composition without first satisfying himself of its aesthetic justification.

After recovering from influenza, he felt able to undertake only light tasks. He rescored part of *The Firebird* as a suite for smaller orchestra, in the hope of encouraging more performances. He wrote another set, which was to be his last, of four songs to Russian folk-poems.

In the spring of 1919 he went to Paris to see Diaghilev, whom he had not met for over a year. He found, however, that his own enthusiasm for *Histoire du soldat* was countered by a bland indifference, even jealousy, on Diaghilev's part. It had been produced independently of Diaghilev's guiding hand: it was not a true Russian work. Now Diaghilev had to entice his lost sheep away from his 'Alpine colleagues', and back into the fold. He tried to do this by proposing a fresh production of *Chant du Rossignol*, with sets and costumes by Henri Matisse, and choreography by Massine. But Stravinsky considered his *Chant du Rossignol* to be best suited to the concert hall; he had called it specifically a symphonic poem. His view was confirmed when Ansermet conducted it in Geneva on 6th December that year.

So Diaghilev made another proposal, which this time found a much readier response from Stravinsky. As *The Good-humoured Ladies*, to Scarlatti's music, and the Cimarosa-Respighi *Astuzie Feminini*, had already proved so successful, would it not be possible to produce a third 'Neapolitan' ballet, with the music of another early Italian composer, Pergolesi? Moreover Picasso and Massine would be his collaborators for the design and choreography respectively. This time the bait proved irresistible. Although the commission meant that he would have to turn his back on his recent innovations, such as the use of small ensembles, and the discovery of jazz, and that he would have to acquaint himself instead with the unfamiliar world of the eighteenth-century Italian baroque style, nevertheless he agreed.

He spent the rest of that year, and the first months of 1920, on the score of *Pulcinella*. But while he immersed himself in the eighteenth-century world, he allowed himself an occasional glance in other directions. *Piano-Rag-Music* continued in the same vein as the ragtime in *Histoire du soldat*; and in the autumn of 1919 Werner Reinhart arranged concerts in Geneva, Lausanne and Zürich of some of the Russian songs and instrumental works of the war years.

The work required for *Pulcinella* appealed to a different side of Stravinsky's creative personality than anything he had hitherto written. He was not so much composing original music, or reinterpreting a particular idiom or style, such as jazz, in his own way, as assimilating and recomposing incomplete fragments of early music. It was to prove the first of many such backward glances. The exact opposite of academic pastiche—a composer is not a scholar—it was a task which appealed immensely to Stravinsky, since it was so suited to his insatiable musicianship. Moreover a similar challenge faced Massine and Picasso, and it proved to be one to which they were fully and agreeably equal. Music, design and choreography blended and matched; their respective creators had fun.

Pulcinella was produced on 15th May 1920 at the Paris Opera House. It proved to be the swan song of Stravinsky's Swiss years. The following month he left Switzerland and settled in France. He spent the summer at Carantec in Brittany, and later moved to Garches near Paris. The isolation of the war years was now over; and indeed this move was to mark the close of one period and the beginning of a fresh one in his life and work.

Paris had been the focal point of the *Ballets Russes* up to then. Five of Stravinsky's main works had been premièred in Paris; he was known to the musical and artistic élite of that city. Moreover, as he says, it was in France at that time, and particularly in Paris, that 'the pulse of the world was throbbing most strongly'.

4   The last of the Russian works

Stravinsky had made many friends during his years in the Vaud country. As well as Ramuz and Ansermet, he met several performers, including the Flonzaley String Quartet. They had already played his *Three pieces for String Quartet*; now they suggested a longer piece. So Stravinsky wrote the *Concertino*, a one-movement work, with a central cadenza for the first violin.

While still in Brittany in the summer of 1920 he also began another instrumental work. The *Revue Musicale* proposed to issue a special number in December in memory of Debussy, who died on 25th March 1918. Stravinsky was among those asked to contribute, and his contribution consisted of a page of piano transcription; a wordless chorale, which later formed the ending of *Symphonies of Wind Instruments*. The easy piano pieces *Les cinq doigts* completed his output that year. Meanwhile, in December, Diaghilev mounted a fresh version of *Le Sacre du printemps*, at the same theatre as the première seven years before, the Théâtre des Champs Élysées; but this time with Massine's choreography, which proved much more successful than Nijinsky's.

In the spring of 1921 Diaghilev included *Petrushka*, which Stravinsky conducted, in his season at Madrid. The two thereafter spent Easter at Seville, and were much taken with the Holy Week processions. After that Stravinsky spent some time in London, where further performances of *Le Sacre* were given in June. In London also Koussevitzky conducted the first performance, on 10th June, of the newly completed *Symphonies of Wind Instruments* in Queen's Hall; but with the twenty-three players at the back of the platform, and the conductor at the front, no rapport was established. It was not a happy occasion; but Stravinsky's attention soon went elsewhere.

With the success of the revivals of this season, and the re-establishment of the *Ballets Russes* after the disruption of the war years, Diaghilev was now able to consider fresh ventures. Two were of concern to Stravinsky. It had been a long-standing wish of Diaghilev to produce that *chef d'œuvre* of Russian classical ballet, Tchaikovsky's *The Sleeping Beauty*. On examining a score, which was obtained from Russia only with great difficulty, it was found that certain parts, which were cut out of the first St Petersburg production, but which Diaghilev now wanted to include, only existed in the piano arrangement. Stravinsky undertook to orchestrate them; also to arrange certain transitions.

The second proposal, which eventually became the opera *Mavra*, arose from the common admiration both Diaghilev and Stravinsky had for the Russian poet Pushkin. This one-act *opera buffa* was taken from Pushkin's rhymed story *The little house in Kolomna*, and the libretto in verse was written by the young Russian poet Boris Kochno, who soon became an active collaborator with Diaghilev. Stravinsky saw himself not in the narrowly nationalist line of 'The Five', but in the truly cosmopolitan tradition of Pushkin, Glinka and Tchaikovsky, to whose memory *Mavra* is dedicated.

On 2nd November 1921 Diaghilev presented his revival of *The Sleeping Beauty* in London. He had prepared it with the utmost care, entrusting Bakst with the scenery and costumes, Sergeyev and Bronislava Nijinska (Nijinsky's sister) with the choreography. It created a profound impression, not least on Stravinsky himself, whose ideal of classical beauty and *ordonnance* was reinforced by what he witnessed. The Apollonian and Dionysian principles [1] of his aesthetic were confirmed in his mind on this occasion. It was with the image of the classical dignity of this work and the unaffected Russian-ness of its creator as his model, that he wrote *Mavra* at Biarritz; he completed it early in March 1922.

That year witnessed another important première for him. This was *Renard*, which on 18th May Princess Polignac generously allowed Diaghilev to produce, and also contributed towards the cost. Ansermet conducted, and Nijinska both danced the title-role and created the athletic choreography. It satisfied Stravinsky musically and scenically, but the burlesque proved too short and too intimate for the wide expanse of the Paris Opéra. It would have been better suited to a soirée, as originally intended by Princess Polignac—of the sort indeed which Diaghilev arranged to introduce *Mavra*, with Stravinsky accompanying on the piano. Unfortunately the first full performance of this opera on 3rd June 1922 was an occasion of acute anti-climax. In seeking to recapture the spirit of freshness and spontaneity of the Italo-Russian school, and to rediscover the old Russian comic opera of Glinka and Dargomijsky, Stravinsky failed to interest a contemporary audience, who were expecting to hear something akin to *Le Sacre* or *Petrushka*. The work was devoid even of the *succès de scandale* that had attended *Le Sacre du printemps*. It failed to shock, or amuse; it failed to rouse interest; even the set was by an unknown artist, Survage. It was dismissed by critics of every shade as unworthy of closer examination. Even Ravel turned his back on Stravinsky after *Mavra*. Diaghilev, annoyed at this failure, asked Stravinsky to alter the ending, which the latter, not unexpectedly, refused to do. Very few realized that it marked a positive turning point in the evolution of Stravinsky's musical thought, which might be described not as neo-classicism so much as a fresh attitude towards the classical aesthetic.

[1] See p. 147.

The score of *Mavra* relied heavily on the wind instruments of the orchestra; taken with the *Symphonies*, this showed the way in which Stravinsky's attention was now moving. His next piece, the *Octet for wind instruments*, was a continuation of this trend; it also represented Stravinsky's preoccupation at this time with structure in an instrumental piece, which was not incidental music, like *Historie du soldat*, but absolute music, a piece in its own right.

Stravinsky's complex, yet strict, aesthetic demands close inspection, and belongs to a later chapter; but it directly affected his life and career, in so far as he regarded the sort of 'interpretation' that is associated with most individual conductors as seriously detrimental to the realization of the true nature of his music. From this moment onwards, therefore, he became more and more his own executant. The *Octuor* was his first concert work that he himself conducted. The unsatisfactory performance of the *Symphonies of Wind Instruments* was partly the reason; the other decisive factor in this development was financial; much-needed fees could be earned by performing, more than from composition.

Meanwhile another stage première was planned by Diaghilev for the following year, 1923, when he decided to produce *Les Noces*. After several abortive attempts to complete the instrumentation of this work, which caused him much thought, Stravinsky had laid it aside unfinished nearly four years earlier. Now, with a deadline to work to, he took the decisive step, and completed the final instrumentation, using the unusual ensemble of four pianos and percussion instruments, on 6th April 1923—a month before the *Octuor*.

The first performance of *Les Noces* was on 13th June in Paris, though, as with *Mavra*, it was preceded the night before by a private performance at the house of Princess Polignac. Much to Diaghilev's relief, after the fiasco of *Mavra* the year before, the work was well received, though Stravinsky's idea that it should be a *divertissement*, like *Histoire du soldat*, with the orchestra on stage, did not find favour with him, and was not carried out.

This was the last time Stravinsky was to use Russian material; indeed, since most of the vocal material of *Les Noces* belonged to the war years, and only the completion of the score dated from 1923, the last of the 'Russian works' was, in effect, *Mavra*. From now on Stravinsky was to seek wider and deeper for sources of inspiration. His severance from Russia affected his creative work as much as his personal affairs. He faced a crisis as a composer, which took several years, and all the exercise of his speculative powers, for him to overcome. He describes these years as a 'decade of samplings, experiments, amalgamations'— an apt summary of the twentieth-century situation.

5 A new classicism

It was after *Les Noces* that the pattern of Stravinsky's work began to change. Since his first association with Diaghilev his greatest achievements had been primarily in the theatre; indeed of the nine stage works up to *Les Noces*, seven had been written specifically for Diaghilev, and eight had been performed for the first time by his company. In most cases Stravinsky made suites, or other transcriptions, for concert use. But *Les Noces* proved to be the last work that he wrote for his friend Diaghilev. Partly this was due to the problem of language. He was cut off from his mother tongue, Russian, and he had not yet assimilated the language of his newly adopted country, France. The *Octuor*, whose première he conducted in Paris on 18th October 1923, was dedicated to Vera de Bosset, and modelled on an eighteenth-century serenade; thereafter he focused his attention more on purely instrumental music. It was to be three years before he wrote another dramatic work.

He was by far the brightest star in Diaghilev's galaxy; but curiously this very fact brought its own diminishing returns, since he became increasingly in demand in Europe and America. Concert appearances fill most of the pages of this part of his *Chronicles*. Whether as conductor or pianist, he spent more and more time on tour, and travelling.

With this purpose in mind he wrote the *Piano Concerto* and, following the preference shown in the two previous instrumental works, confined the orchestra to the wind instruments, with double basses. It was first heard at a private gathering at Princess

Polignac's in May 1924, with the orchestral part played on a second piano. Stravinsky had always been a pianist, ever since the early years when he worked in St Petersburg as an accompanist.[1] Indeed he invariably composed at the piano; he described the piano as 'the fulcrum of all my musical discoveries'. But he did not seek the career of a concert virtuoso. He was modest about his left-hand technique; moreover he was not interested in developing the memory of a concert pianist. His composer's mind was too sharp, his imagination too acute and selective, to permit him to 'memorize, automatically and simply, like a camera'. Indeed at the public première of the *Piano Concerto,* on 22nd May 1924, the conductor, Koussevitzky, had to hum the first notes of the Largo when Stravinsky suffered a momentary lapse of memory.

The success of the *Concerto,* and his concern with purely instrumental music, particularly for the piano, also 'the instruction principle of eighteenth-century classicism', prompted his next work, the *Piano Sonata.* This occupied his last months at Biarritz, before moving to Nice. Not only was Nice sheltered from the Atlantic gales, but Cocteau lived near by. Stravinsky lived there until 1931. After completing the *Piano Sonata,* in Nice, he immediately set out on a European concert tour.

Early in 1925 he first appeared in America, as pianist and conductor—nine years after Diaghilev's war-time tour, when he had been compelled to stay in Switzerland. Now he was greeted with 'full houses and acclamations'. On his return, Barcelona, Rome, Paris in their turn greeted him with concerts, festivals and fresh ballet productions—including Diaghilev's new version of *Chant du Rossignol,* with Balanchine's choreography.

Back in Nice for the summer he continued an already begun *Serenade in A* for piano—the length of which was decided by a

---

[1] To a cellist, Eugene Malmgreen, whose niece, Vera de Bosset, later became his second wife.

recording contract that he had won in America. Each of its movements was intended to fill one side of a record. In the event, it was to prove an admirable companion piece to the still-unperformed *Sonata*. Less weighty than the *Sonata*, its motivation was equally classical—this time 'in imitation of the *Nachtmusik* of the eighteenth century'.

No sooner was this completed than he was off again on his travels. He played the *Sonata* first at Donaueschingen in July, later at an I.S.C.M. Festival in Venice on 8th September. There, whether by accident or design, he narrowly missed meeting Schoenberg, who conducted his *Serenade* at a concert the day before. His friend Princess Polignac was in Venice for that event, and her *salon* attracted, as usual, the musical and intellectual élite.

The desire that had been at the back of Stravinsky's mind for several years, to write another large stage-work, now became more urgently felt. The problem of which language to choose caused him much anxiety, but it was solved by chance when, on his way back from Venice, he stopped in Genoa, where he happened to buy a life of St Francis of Assisi. Reading this served to confirm his idea that a text for music might be endowed with a certain timeless, monumental quality by being translated from a secular to a sacred language. The saint's everyday language was Italian, but for hieratic, poetic use he used Provençal. For his work Stravinsky decided to use not the everyday language of French or German but the timeless, sublime language of Latin.

For his subject he took, not the world of fairy-stories, or tales of old Russia, but the familiar myths of classical Greece. In this, he was following the example set by other contemporary composers, such as Milhaud and Honegger. He consulted Cocteau, whose *Antigone* had recently much impressed him; and together they decided on *Oedipus Rex*. Stravinsky had read Sophocles' play, as a boy, in Guedich's translation. Now he and

Cocteau worked on it for two months, before he left for another tour of concerts later in the year. The new work was to be kept as a surprise for Diaghilev, whose twentieth anniversary as a theatrical promoter with the *Ballets Russes* would fall in the spring of 1927. Early in the new year (1926) Stravinsky received part of the libretto from Cocteau, and was able to start work on the new opera-oratorio. This was interrupted in the spring by various concert appearances, including *Le Rossignol* and *Petrushka* at La Scala, Milan. The rest of the year, however, was entirely given over to the new work, which was finished on 14th March 1927.

As it was intended as an anniversary present for Diaghilev, it could hardly be staged without his being aware of it. Diaghilev, therefore, was told only at the last moment, and it was decided to give it as a concert work. Even this entailed a large outlay, which was met only through the generosity of Princess Polignac. She once again paid for a private preview at her house, with Stravinsky accompanying at the piano. The fee was then handed over by Stravinsky to pay for the public première, which took place on 30th May at the Sarah Bernhardt Theatre.

As usual, Stravinsky's æsthetic pattern for this piece was as precise as it was original. The idea of the speaker, which was Cocteau's, might recall *Histoire du soldat*, but in retrospect Stravinsky was to regard the speaker's passages as unjustified 'interruptions', and some of Cocteau's phrases as intolerable. It is an 'opera-oratorio' because the participants address not each other but the audience, and there is no operatic movement. At a later production, in 1952, Cocteau introduced huge masks and symbolic mime—all of which worked in very well with Stravinsky's carefully graded score. But the première was not fully successful ('un cadeau très macabre' was Diaghilev's rueful description), partly because it sounded grim and austere when juxtaposed to that most colourful of his ballets, *The Firebird*. As so often with new Stravinsky works, no one knew what to expect. But it is a work which requires stage presentation, since the music and the dramatic situation develop in parallel.

Shortly afterwards Stravinsky received a commission for another ballet from the American patron Mrs Elizabeth Sprague Coolidge. It was to be performed in the Library of Congress. The choice of another classical subject was natural after *Oedipus Rex*, and he set about composing a half-hour work 'founded on episodes of Greek mythology plastically interpreted by dancing of the so-called classical school'. His theme was *Apollo Musagetes* —Apollo, Master of the Muses—here reduced from their original nine to the three who most characteristically represented the choreographic art: Calliope, who personifies the rhythm of poetry; Polyhymnia, who personifies mime, the narrative of gesture; and Terpsichore, who takes place of honour as the revealer of dance.

Stravinsky's score consists of a series of allegorical dances, preceded by a prologue representing the birth of Apollo, and followed by an apotheosis in which Apollo leads Terpsichore to Parnassus, where they live for ever afterwards. Stravinsky admired particularly the beauty of line in classical dancing, and had in mind 'white ballet', in which the art is revealed in all its purity, without dramatic conflicts or contrasts. For this reason he adopted a diatonic style, and used an orchestra of strings only, excluding the heterogeneous sonorities of brass, wind and percussion. The contrasts are therefore of dynamics, not of instrumental colour. By these means, which were in marked contrast with his recent instrumental work, Stravinsky was consciously striving after that melodic principle for which, as he saw it, the strings were originally intended in their country of origin, Italy. After writing several works for the wind instruments, it was a pleasure for him to immerse himself in the sonorous euphony of strings. The orchestra is in six parts, with divided violoncelli, made for sharpness and clarity. Thus he clothed the main idea of the work, which is a study in 'versification'; variations on iambic (reversed dot) rhythm patterns or musical Alexandrines. The *pas d'action* is the only dance variation in which patterns of iambic stress are not immediately apparent. In this work, which was a tribute to seventeenth-century France, Stravinsky worked towards a long-line polyphonic style, which was to prove a storehouse for later works. The score was finished early in 1928.

After the first performance in Washington on 27th April the composer conducted a performance with Diaghilev's company in Paris two months later, with Sergey Lifar as Apollo, and choreography by the twenty-four-year-old George Balanchine, the brilliant young choreographer for whom this event was a turning point in his career. The work was well received, though the critics, expecting one thing and hearing another, expressed varying degrees of incomprehension.

Apollo is a landmark for another less happy reason; it was the last work of Stravinsky's to be produced by Diaghilev's *Ballets Russes*. The autumn and winter of that year were spent by the composer on work for another ballet, but this time one that was commissioned by Ida Rubinstein, a wealthy actress and dancer who was just inaugurating a new company, and who wished to build a repertory. The proposal, put by the painter Alexandre Benois, who worked with her, was for a work inspired by the music of Tchaikovsky. Not only was Stravinsky's admiration for Tchaikovsky's music well known, but November 1928, when the new work would be performed, happened to be also the thirty-fifth anniversary of his death.

Both subject and scenario were left for Stravinsky to choose, and he went to an author whose imagination and sense of the fantastic seemed to be akin to those of Tchaikovsky, an author moreover whom Stravinsky had already made use of in *Le Rossignol*—Hans Andersen. He chose the story of *The Ice Maiden*, and decided to build the ballet round selections from Tchaikovsky's music. He renamed the work *The Fairy's Kiss* and, as with *Apollo*, he visualized the classical style of 'white ballet'. Time was short, and he was only just able to finish the orchestration by November. He was not able to attend to the choreography which Bronislava Nijinska prepared. In the event he was not satisfied with the result; but he was not able to affect it materially before the première, which he conducted at the Paris Opera House on 27th November.

The production of *The Fairy's Kiss* marked the final breach with Diaghilev, who took it amiss that Stravinsky should accept a commission from another company than his own. Ida Rubinstein had been a dancer with the *Ballets Russes*; her performance in *Sheherazade* had been spectacular; nevertheless this did nothing to mollify Diaghilev's wrathful indignation, as he proceeded to vilify and demolish *The Fairy's Kiss* and everything to do with it. But the resulting breach between Stravinsky and Diaghilev was caused merely by outward events, not by any deep, inner antipathy. On the contrary, the ties which united them, ties of nationality and creative achievement, were indissoluble. The creation of the *Ballets Russes* was due to Diaghilev; its success was in large measure due to Stravinsky.

Three of Stravinsky's stage works up to 1929 were written independently of Diaghilev; *Histoire du soldat*, *Apollo* and *The Fairy's Kiss*. Only the second of these was produced by the *Ballets Russes*, and even then, although Diaghilev seems to have been genuinely moved by the music, he wanted to make an alteration in the score.[1] But Stravinsky never forgot the debt he owed to Diaghilev from the early days in St Petersburg; equally, Diaghilev's confidence in the music of his chief protégé never wavered, right up to the final performance of *Le Sacre* in London in July 1929. This was his company's last season; on 19th August Diaghilev died in Venice, and Stravinsky gave himself up to grief.

[1] To omit the Terpsichore variation, or to shorten it.

Diaghilev's death was not only a personal loss to Stravinsky; it left a void which could not be, and has not been, filled. The chief testament to his greatness, and the power of his judgement, is the work of Stravinsky himself, which had been moulded and shaped by the *Ballets Russes*. Now he was compelled to turn elsewhere. His friend the conductor Ansermet had started a new orchestra in Paris in 1928, the Orchestre Symphonique de Paris, and Stravinsky was invited to conduct two concerts during their first season. It was with these players in mind that he directed his attention towards his next work, a piece for piano and orchestra, which he himself would play. His earlier *Concerto* had proved most successful; indeed, over recent years he had received some forty invitations to play it. It was time, therefore, to write another, and reserve exclusive performing rights for five years. The new one, which he called *Capriccio*, occupied most of 1929, interspersed with public appearances. It was finished at the end of September, and he gave the première at the Salle Pleyel on 6th December, with Ansermet conducting his new orchestra. It subsequently proved to be as much in demand as the *Concerto*, and thereafter Stravinsky performed it frequently, both as soloist and conductor. It was in a performance of this piece in Barcelona, conducted by him four years later, that his younger son Soulima made his début as a pianist.

Meanwhile another major work was commissioned from Stravinsky, by the Boston Symphony Orchestra under their conductor Koussevitzky. He had links with the organization since 1914 when Monteux left the Diaghilev company to become their principal conductor. The form of the new work caused Stravinsky much thought. The idea of a large-scale symphonic piece had been in his mind for a long time, but he was not attracted by symphonic form as bequeathed by the nineteenth century. His work would not conform to the conventions of sonata form; on the other hand he wanted to create an organic whole, and develop it contrapuntally. In the event, the ensemble built up for the *Symphony of Psalms* consists of a choral and instrumental section, each treated independently and equally. As in the *Piano Concerto*, he discards the upper strings of the orchestra; in the *Symphony of Psalms* only cellos and basses appear; no clarinets, but five flutes and five oboes; in the choir, children's voices are preferred to sopranos and contraltos. For the text he sought a universal theme—his interpretation of the publisher's request for something 'popular'—in words written for singing. The same reasons prompted him to take a Latin text as had swayed him before with *Oedipus Rex*.

The *Symphony of Psalms*, the first of several large-scale religious works, occupied Stravinsky until the summer of 1930, with the now customary interruptions for concert tours. It was first heard in Brussels on 13th December, conducted by Ansermet; Koussevitzky conducted the American première in Boston six days later.

The following year an important fresh element was infused into Stravinsky's work, which caused him to turn his attention to writing for the solo violin. It came about through Willy Strecker, head of the German publishers Schott's Söhne of Mainz. Since 1912, starting with *Petrushka*, the greater part of Stravinsky's music was published by the Édition Russe, founded by Serge Koussevitzky, and his wife Natalie. The London firm of J. & W. Chester also acquired certain rights in 1920. Now by 1930 Stravinsky's fame, as composer and executant, had become world wide; it is not altogether surprising that another publisher should vie for his services.

After a concert in Wiesbaden, Strecker introduced Stravinsky to the violinist Samuel Dushkin, and after some appropriate mutual hesitation, it was not long before a violin concerto was planned, to a commission from Dushkin's American patron Blair Fairchild. Stravinsky had written for the violin already; *Histoire du soldat* and the *Concertino* contained extensive solo writing, as did the cadenza in *Apollo*; but he had never looked on the violin as a potential solo instrument in the same way as he did the piano—which he himself played and understood. He also consulted Hindemith, whose close acquaintance he made at this time through Strecker, though he had met him earlier; whereupon, with the active co-operation of Dushkin, he set about his task, and began the *Violin Concerto* early in 1931. He treated the violin as a solo instrument in combination, and omitted a cadenza for this reason.

Interruptions to the composition were caused not only by concert appearances but by a family move in the summer from Nice, where they had lived since 1924, to Voreppe, near Grenoble. The new concerto was first played by Dushkin in Berlin on 23rd October 1931—the first of Stravinsky's works to have a German première—and repeated elsewhere in November and December.

Stravinsky's interest in the violin was stimulated rather than satisfied by the concerto, and it was not long before he embarked on another piece, partly to explore the possibilities of the instrument, partly with a view to concert tours with Dushkin. So he wrote the *Duo Concertant*. As with the concerto, he had in mind chiefly the possibilities of combining the two instruments, violin and piano. The work was finished by 15th July 1932, and after its première on 28th October, also in Berlin, he and Dushkin went on tour, playing as well as the *Duo* several transcriptions for violin and piano from stage works, which Stravinsky made at about this time.[1] The first tour was a success, and they made another one the following season, 1933–4, and thereafter.

After this spate of violin composition Stravinsky's attention was brought back to the theatre, and to Paris, when Ida Rubinstein approached him with an idea for another ballet. After the death of Diaghilev in 1929 the *Ballets Russes* became ineffective; Ida Rubinstein's company therefore took a leading position in

[1] See Appendix B, pp. 175–6.

Paris. Her ideas for *Persephone* were complex. As well as casting herself in the leading role, she saw the ballet as a combination of speech, song, dance and mime. Stravinsky later described it as a 'masque co-ordinated with a sung and spoken text'.

The chosen text was a 'Hymn to Demeter', written before the war by André Gide. Gide and Stravinsky, who had known each other since 1910, met in February 1933 in Wiesbaden, and the first steps towards the new collaboration proceeded with great cordiality. Gide rewrote his original *Persephone* after this meeting. But if the classical subject-matter was familiar ground to the composer, the setting of a French text was not. He had studiously avoided it since the Verlaine songs of 1910; and although he had lived in France for many years, and was shortly to become a French citizen, he never again set French words to music. In the event, his setting of the words of *Persephone*, though pleasing to him, appeared to Gide to violate the basic rules of prosody. 'C'est curieux, c'est très curieux' was his comment on first hearing the music. Moreover, he differed with the composer over several points of libretto and production, and was not present at the rehearsals or the first performance on 30th April 1934, though he did attend the unstaged preview at Princess Polignac's. Stravinsky did not take kindly to such overt disapproval, and the partnership inevitably deteriorated. His later view, that W. H. Auden should be commissioned 'to fit the music with new words', is the measure of this deterioration. But the difference between the two was political and religious as well as artistic. Though he later changed, Gide was then a sympathetic supporter of Stalin's communism; Stravinsky's viewpoint, as a White Russian, was very different.

Gide's view, though he later recanted, was expressed in a message to the Congress of Soviet Writers in 1935:

On the high road of history on which each country must sooner or later travel, the Soviet Union has taken the lead in a glorious manner.

Stravinsky's view, expressed in *The Poetics of Music* in 1939, was:

> If the reeling of Russia through the course of history disorients me to the point of making my head swim, the perspectives of Russian musical art disconcert me no less. For art presupposes a culture, an upbringing, an integral stability of the intellect, and Russia of today has never been more completely devoid of these.

On 10th June 1934 Stravinsky became a French citizen. Towards the end of the year he moved from Voreppe to Paris, where he remained for five years. The following year he asserted his citizenship in several ways; first by publishing his memoirs in French (*Chroniques de ma vie*); next by applying for membership of the Institut de France, in place of Paul Dukas. This was on Valéry's suggestion; but he lost the election to Florent Schmitt. Further time that year was taken up on another American tour, which he shared with Dushkin; the only new composition of that year—although it is a substantial and important work—is the *Concerto for two solo pianos*. Stravinsky wrote it, without commission, for himself and his son Soulima, using a special double piano built by Pleyel: a concerto without orchestra. Together they presented the première in Paris on 21st November 1935; Soulima had appeared in the *Capriccio* two years earlier, and was already becoming known, largely through his playing of his father's works.

The success of the *Duo Concertant* for violin and piano led Stravinsky to write a double concerto for two pianos, but within the framework of chamber music and not requiring full orchestra. Soulima played the piano suite from *Petrushka* at the same concert as the new concerto; both works were introduced by Stravinsky in a fifteen-minute talk. The two went on a tour of Europe and South America in 1936.

Though his fame, and the demand for his concert appearances, might not suggest it, Stravinsky was aware at this time of his growing estrangement from a large section of the public. He had enjoyed acclaim at an early age, when most composers are still struggling to make themselves heard; his early ballets, thanks to Diaghilev, had enjoyed a unique, worldwide success. Now, however, some of the public who heard and applauded the Russian ballets were not able to follow Stravinsky into the concert hall. He says, prophetically, at the end of his *Chronicles*, writing in 1935: 'They cannot follow me in the progress of my musical thought. What moves and delights me leaves them indifferent, and what still continues to interest them holds no further attraction for me.'

Stravinsky's art is dynamic, not static. From the very earliest days in St Petersburg, he was incapable of repeating himself; each work explored or developed some new territory. No doubt this was disconcerting for his audiences, to say nothing of his imitators and critics, who would become accustomed to the style of one work only in time to discover that its creator had moved on to the next.

6 A fresh start

During 1936, as well as concert tours with Soulima and other activities, another idea was already forming in Stravinsky's mind; indeed it had been forming over some ten years. This was for a ballet in which dancers, dressed as playing cards, performed against a gaming-table backdrop of green baize. *Jeu de cartes* (The Card Party), is concerned with three deals of poker, with the joker as principal dancer; the composer himself, an inveterate card-player since he first played *durachki* as a child, now frequently regaled his rest periods between composition with games of poker. Though written mainly in Paris, the work is 'Germanic' in style, no doubt partly as a result of his concert-links with Germany established through Strecker; and the work was destined to have more success in that country, even in the Hitler years just before the war.

After the disbandment of the *Ballets Russes*, one of the most prominent ballet companies in France was Ida Rubinstein's; but in America a fresh start was made with the founding of Lincoln Kirstein's American Ballet. George Balanchine was his choreographer. When Kirstein commissioned *Jeu de cartes* for production in New York by his newly formed company, to Balanchine's choreography, Stravinsky was already a familiar figure on the American concert scene. This was not his first American commission; but it was the first important score the American première of which he himself conducted—on 27th April 1937 at the Metropolitan Opera House. The evening also included *Apollo*, and Balanchine's new version of *The Fairy's*

43

Kiss. The political instability in Europe at this time, the gloomy possibility of a future war, and his estrangement from his former public, all caused the composer to stay longer and look closer at the apparently brighter American scene than he had previously. Already on his second American tour in 1935 he had thought of living in Los Angeles; so now once again his itinerary included Hollywood. It also took him to Washington, D.C., where Robert Woods Bliss and his wife invited him to write a *Concerto Grosso*, to be played the next year at their nearby estate, Dumbarton Oaks, in celebration of their thirtieth wedding anniversary.[1]

On his return to Europe, Stravinsky moved from Paris to Annemasse, near Geneva, to be near his wife, Catherine, and two daughters, Ludmilla and Milena, who were confined to a sanatorium with tuberculosis. This was the 'family disease', which also struck him. He was recommended to have treatment just after *Jeu de cartes*. It was in the shadow of this illness that he wrote the *Dumbarton Oaks Concerto*. No sooner was it finished, in the spring of 1938, than two other commissions reached him from America. The first, once again from Mrs Bliss, was for nothing less than a symphony, in celebration of the fiftieth season of the Chicago Symphony Orchestra in 1940–1941; the second, from Harvard University, invited him to accept the Charles Eliot Norton Chair of Poetry, 1939–40, and to deliver in that time six lectures on music.

The first commission led to the *Symphony in C,* his second symphony, which he began in the autumn of 1938. Work was interrupted in November for a concert tour of Italy; and it was after a stay in Rome that he heard of the sudden deterioration of his daughter Ludmilla. She died on 30th November. Stravinsky's grief was intense, and tolerable only through his becoming immersed in work on the new Symphony.

[1] This house was also to be the setting, in the autumn of 1944, for the international conference at which the idea of the United Nations was first put forward.

Nor was this all. Three months later, on 2nd March 1939, his wife Catherine also died of the same disease. As a result he decided to undergo treatment himself; a New York doctor had already made a positive diagnosis in his case also. He spent five months of 1939 at the sanatorium at Sancellemoz, where his younger daughter Milena was already a patient (she was to have treatment for six years). During these months the second movement of the *Symphony in C* was written. On 7th June yet a third bereavement occurred, when Stravinsky's mother died; for the third time within seven months he 'endured the long Russian Requiem service' for one of his own family.

Meanwhile in the sanatorium he began to turn his attention towards the second commission, and the lectures he was to deliver later in the year at Harvard. He discussed the project with his old friend Souvtchinsky, who 'fed books' to him, and helped him draft the lectures in Russian. Roland-Manuel prepared the French text.

This was an unhappy period of Stravinsky's life. Not only was he aware of that decline in public interest in his recent music that he had remarked on four years previously, but the years just before the war marked a fall-off in his European concert tours. The ever-increasing political tension, and the loss of three close members of his own family within so short a space, also served to cause him to seek release from the stress and irritations of Europe, and to seek for haven, as well as a better-ordered new life, in America; which he did in September, at the outbreak of war.

He landed in New York on 30th September, and went straight to Cambridge, Massachusetts. The six Harvard lectures were later published under the title *The Poetics of Music*; they form the basis of a consideration of Stravinsky's aesthetic.[1] While at Harvard he completed the third movement of the *Symphony in*

[1] See p. 146.

C; he also directed Walter Piston's composition seminar in some analysis classes, in which he discussed and demonstrated his own recent work, as well as that of young composers. He had previously taken part in such class demonstrations with Nadia Boulanger at the École Normale in Paris four years earlier.

After some concerts in Los Angeles in December 1939 he returned to New York, where Vera de Bosset arrived from Genoa on 13th January, 1940. They had been close acquaintances for many years, and were married in Boston, Massachusetts, on 9th March. Eventually, after travelling extensively, the couple reached Los Angeles, where Stravinsky, at the age of fifty-eight, had now decided to begin his new life.

His first work was to complete the much-interrupted *Symphony in C*. This was done on 19th August, just in time for the première in Chicago on 7th November, conducted by the composer. In the event, and in spite of its being avoided by younger conductors, the work proved a turning-point in Stravinsky's output. Two years later he began another symphony, his third; but meanwhile other less weighty tasks befell him.

During these war years Hollywood was a cosmopolitan city, which, according to Thomas Mann, was 'more intellectually stimulating than Paris or Munich had ever been'. Apart from Mann, and literary figures such as Aldous Huxley and Franz Werfel, Stravinsky found himself in the company of Alexandre Tansman, Nadia Boulanger and Adolph Bolm. There was a ferment of composers, writers, scientists, artists, actors, philosophers, and 'genuine phoneys'. His near-neighbour was Arnold Schoenberg, though the two were temperamentally incompatible and rarely met. They were confronted with each other, for the first time since the Berlin performance of *Pierrot Lunaire* in 1912, at Franz Werfel's funeral in 1945, when Stravinsky admits to his being impressed by 'the angry, tortured, burning face of Arnold Schoenberg'.

As he was now living in Hollywood it was inevitable that sooner or later someone would ask him for a film score. The previous December he had seen Walt Disney's *Fantasia,* and had witnessed the execrable treatment meted out to sections of *Le Sacre du printemps.* Now he was to witness at first hand the irreconcileable claims of commerce and art. He was offered $100,000 to 'pad a film with music'; when he refused, he was offered the same money if he would allow somebody else to compose the music in his name.

Stravinsky had no illusions about film-music; nevertheless some film-projects did lead him to write small scores. A projected film about the Nazi invasion of Norway led eventually to the *Four Norwegian Moods* (1942), in which he incorporated themes from a collection of Norwegian folk-music which he and Vera found in Los Angeles. The *Scherzo à la Russe* began as music for another war film, with a Russian setting; it was then used for a commission from the band-leader Paul Whiteman, before being rescored for orchestra.

Orson Welles urged him to compose music for his film *Jane Eyre*; Stravinsky wrote a piece for one of the hunting scenes, which was finally used as the 'Eclogue' middle movement of his orchestral *Ode* (1943), when no agreement was reached on terms of the contract for the film. Franz Werfel also asked Stravinsky to contribute music to his film *Song of Bernadette*; again the terms of the contract appeared to the ever-watchful composer to be 'too much in the producer's favour', and he used the music he had up to then written, for the 'Apparition of the Virgin' scene, as the middle movement of his next symphony.

Apart from these slight contacts with film-makers, which came to nothing, Stravinsky wrote several other scores in these early years in Hollywood. The *Tango* for piano, later scored for orchestra, dates from 1940. The following year he was commissioned by the Werner Janssen Orchestra of Los Angeles to write a concert piece for a chamber orchestra of twenty-four players.

47

The result was *Danses Concertantes*, a five-movement suite conceived as an abstract ballet.

Some of the invitations that he received can only be described as bizarre. *Circus Polka* resulted from a telephone call from George Balanchine one day in 1942:

Balanchine: Voudriez-vous me composer un ballet?
Stravinsky: Pour qui?
Balanchine: Pour des éléphants.
Stravinsky: Quel âge?
Balanchine: Très jeunes.
Stravinsky: Alors, entendu!

The resulting four-minute piece was first heard under the Big Top, played by the Barnum and Bailey Circus Band.

Two years later the cantata *Babel* was written as the result of another unusual project. A publisher, Nathaniel Shilkret, wished to bring out a seven-movement cycle of pieces by seven different composers, depicting various scenes and moods from the Book of Genesis. From this singularly unpromising proposal Stravinsky culled virtue, and his seven-minute *Babel* for narrator, male-voice chorus and orchestra takes its place in the chain of religious works that from now on gradually increased in number and range. For the first time, moreover, he used an English text; and this was something that had been his intention since arriving in America. The *Ode*, which was first heard on 8th October 1943 in Boston, was commissioned by Stravinsky's old friend and champion Koussevitzky, in memory of his wife Natalie who had just died.

The circumstances that gave rise to *Scènes de Ballet* also had their unusual aspect. Billy Rose was the producer of a Broadway revue, *The Seven Lively Arts*, and he invited Stravinsky to contribute to it with a fifteen-minute ballet suite. There were to be two solo dancers, Alicia Markova and Anton Dolin; Dolin would also compose the choreography. Stravinsky's ideas for the piece were, as usual, most precise; the sequence, character and proportions were his own, and he visualized the dance-construction of this plotless, 'abstract' ballet as he wrote the music. The piece is a period portrait of Broadway in the last years of the war. The 'Apotheosis' movement, recalling *Apollo Musagetes*, pleased the composer most; it was finished in August 1944 as he listened to the radio report of the liberation of Paris, and something of jubilation finds its way into the music.

7   American citizen

On 28th December 1945, Stravinsky became an American citizen; and almost immediately, on 24th January 1946, there took place in New York the première of the *Symphony in three movements*, for which the composer conducted the New York Philharmonic.

The two events are related. While the depiction of pictorial or 'programme' content has no place in Stravinsky's aesthetic, and his music is invariably complete in itself, his musical imagination was excited and aroused by world events. This symphony occupies a position of central importance in Stravinsky's output, partly because it is his testament to the end of the long years of the Second World War, and the tragi-comic spectacle of Hitler's '1,000 year Reich'; partly because it represents the consolidation of riches acquired from many sources, concentrated into one work; also it is the foretaste of future developments in his own style.

The symphony was begun as long ago as 1942. Like *Petrushka* it was started as a concertante work for piano; unlike the *Symphony in C*, the piano is given a prominent part in the instrumental ensemble. The first movement of the symphony was inspired by a war film, a documentary about scorched-earth tactics in China; the third movement even contains a 'war plot', and the square march-beat, the brass-band instrumentation, the grotesque *crescendo* on the tuba, are all related to pictures, which the composer found repellent, of goose-stepping German soldiers. This symphony marked a culminating point in Stravinsky's output for the symphony orchestra. He never wrote another symphonic work on this scale, or of equal intensity.

The first half of 1946 was spent in writing a piece for string orchestra, the *Concerto in D*, which Paul Sacher had asked for to mark the twentieth anniversary of the Basel Chamber Orchestra the following year. After the symphony, it was comparatively lightweight. It was, however, to the theatre that Stravinsky was shortly to return, with two substantial new works. *Orpheus* was commissioned by Lincoln Kirstein for the New York City Ballet; Balanchine was the choreographer. This time, unlike *Jeu de cartes*, he and Stravinsky planned the ballet together from the start. Work at this level must have reminded the sixty-five-year-old composer of the great moments of Diaghilev's old company.

Orpheus was first heard in New York on 28th April 1948, by which time Stravinsky was already well on the way towards his next stage work, the opera *The Rake's Progress*. These two theatre-pieces were separated by the *Mass*, which he finished in March 1948, though the first two sections, *Kyrie* and *Gloria*, were written four years earlier. This work was inspired by something more than Stravinsky's deep-rooted spiritual commitment to Christianity; it was intended to be used liturgically. The accompaniment of ten wind instruments (as in the *Symphony of Psalms*, he avoided using the organ) would proscribe its use in the Orthodox Church, where all musical instruments are forbidden; but by setting the Latin text of the Roman Catholic Mass, Stravinsky hoped that his *Mass* would find a place in Catholic churches. It has, though rarely; the low ebb to which twentieth-century liturgical church music had sunk did not readily admit such works as this by a contemporary composer.

About this time, after 1947, Stravinsky rewrote many pre-1931 works, largely for copyright reasons, as they had been pirated in America. But the work which chiefly occupied him was *The Rake's Progress*, which took three years to write, from

1948 to 1951. The first seeds of the idea were sown when he saw Hogarth's paintings in the Chicago Art Institute in 1947; and in October of that year he wrote to W. H. Auden, on Aldous Huxley's suggestion, and put the proposal of a verse-opera on that theme. Auden went to California in November, when they planned the scenario together; the libretto was ready by 31st March the following year, and Auden delivered it to Stravinsky in a Washington hotel. The latter did not travel to Europe during these years, though his work was interspersed with various conducting engagements in the United States in 1949 and 1950. He wrote approximately one act a year. *The Rake's Progress*, like *Mavra*, is emphatically an opera, not a 'music drama'; its musical structure rests on arias, recitatives, choruses, ensembles; these, and the relations of tonalities, are, as he says, 'in line with the classical tradition'.

Worldwide interest was aroused by the news that Stravinsky was engaged on another opera. It would be his first for thirty years, since *Mavra*. Many opera houses, including the Metropolitan, New York and Covent Garden, vied with each other to present the première; eventually it was decided that it should be given in the comparative intimacy of the Fenice Theatre in Venice; and it was here that Stravinsky conducted the first performance, on 11th September 1951. It was the highlight of an extensive tour of Europe, the first for some time, which kept him away between August and November; *The Rake's Progress* thus began its own progress through the world's opera houses.

After the great exertion and achievement of *The Rake's Progress*, which is his longest single work, it was only to be expected that Stravinsky would allow himself a moment of relaxation before setting out on his next task. Apart from conducting engagements, which brought him back to Europe between April and June the following year, only one work occupied him for the remainder of 1951 and the first half of 1952: the little *Cantata* for soprano, tenor, female chorus and five instruments. The problems of setting English words had fully occupied his attention during *The Rake's Progress*, and now he wished to pursue this, but in a purer, non-dramatic form. He chose four anonymous lyrics of the fifteenth and sixteenth centuries from an anthology edited by W. H. Auden and N. H. Pearson. The piece is a technical study in canon, inversion and retrograde, and one that is prophetic of Stravinsky's future discoveries of style.

In the years leading up to *The Rake's Progress* he was helped by a young American music student who had been at the Juilliard School, Robert Craft, and who soon came to be accepted into the Stravinsky family. He first met Stravinsky on 31st March 1948 in Washington, at the time when W. H. Auden was delivering the completed libretto of *The Rake's Progress*. Over the following years Craft was able to assist with the problems of English pronunciation. In 1948, aged twenty-four, he was a go-ahead young conductor, with a pronounced flair for contemporary music, particularly the second Viennese school, Schoenberg–Berg–Webern, and their latter-day descendants. Later Craft was to publish several volumes of 'conversations' with Stravinsky, as well as his own 'Diaries'. He thus added his name to the considerable list of those who have written valuable first-hand accounts of Stravinsky at various times: Ramuz, Tansman, Nabokov, Ansermet and several others.[1]

Of Stravinsky's children by his first wife Catherine, his younger daughter Milena saw her father regularly and lived near by. She moved to California in 1947 with her husband André Marion, who became Stravinsky's accountant and business manager. His two sons Theodore and Soulima lived separate lives, one in Switzerland, the other in America. Hence over the ensuing years Robert Craft came to be accepted by the Stravinskys not just as a musical assistant but more closely, *in loco filii*.

[1] See Appendix D—Bibliography.

He also assisted as conductor at rehearsals for concerts and recording sessions.

The years following *The Rake's Progress* witness a marked resumption of Stravinsky's conducting engagements. As well as appearing in America every year, unless prevented by illness, he undertook a foreign tour, usually during the summer months. In addition to widening his concert work, he also in these years widened and developed his musical idiom. These were the years when the influence of the second Viennese school began to be chiefly felt in Europe and America, and the tide of serialism began to flood through Western music. Once again Paris was an important focal point of the new development; René Leibowitz propagated the newly-orthodox twelve-note style, while, more important, Messiaen's class at the Conservatoire included many young composers of the next generation, including Boulez, Philippot and Stockhausen.

It is inconceivable that Stravinsky should have remained impervious to such a movement. Everything that affected the *materia musica* was his concern. Just as in 1912 he had recognized and assimilated the central importance of Debussy, and the effect of Debussy on the mainstream of European music, so forty years later he recognized, and identified, the impact of the Viennese school, whose work he assessed with his customary highly developed aesthetic discipline and creative curiosity.

Of the Viennese trinity it was Webern who chiefly interested him. Webern's aesthetic and musical philosophy were closest to his own; it was Webern's ordering of the time element that particularly aroused his sympathy. Composition for Stravinsky consisted partly of a search for order; serialism presented him with nothing less, or more, than a new means to achieve such order. It was not for him a style so much as a discipline. As will be discussed in a later chapter, Stravinsky interpreted serialism in accordance with the same intellectual strictness and rigour that he brought to bear on all other music. Stravinsky the concert-giver was as much concerned as Stravinsky the composer with this extra addition to the Western musical language: 'Developments in language are not easily abandoned, and the composer who fails to take account of them may lose the mainstream.'

Ansermet's introducing Stravinsky to jazz thirty-five years before had resulted in some jazz-inspired work. Now in 1952 it was largely through Craft's introduction that Stravinsky was to hear serial music, and thereafter to use serialism for his own purposes. In January and February 1952 he became particularly familiar with Webern's Quartet, Op. 22; later also that composer's cantatas and songs. Jazz had occupied his attention only momentarily, and had been applied in a few pieces; but serialism was a much weightier and radical matter, concerned as it was with time and structure. From 1953 onwards he strove to adapt and refine it to his own use. He asked himself the searching question: 'Was I merely trying to refit old ships, while the other side—Schoenberg—sought new forms of travel?' The solution he found was both practical and aesthetic—if, indeed, these terms are not interchangeable. Serialism was no artistic *credo* or ossified 'system' to which he became a 'convert', though it appeared so to many at the time; it was an active, evolving art-force, through which he saw the possibility of enriching the scope and depth of his music.

Thus he entered, after *The Rake's Progress*, the second period of crisis in his composing career. The first, after he had been cut off from Russia, had taken several years to surmount, while he sought a solution in a re-application of classical principles; the second, when he 'outgrew the special incubator' in which *The Rake's Progress* had been written, was surmounted in a shorter period of adjustment, while he discovered the principles of Webernian serialism in a 'slow climb through the 1950s'.

His first task after *The Rake's Progress* was to set some more English words. The *Cantata* already mentioned uses anonymous fifteenth- and sixteenth-century lyrics, which appealed for their 'syllabification'. The new paths he began to explore in the twenties had been heralded by the *Octet*; so now, thirty years later, he used a similar piece as a foretaste of what was to come—the *Septet*, in which he first tentatively uses a 'note-row', and begins to break up the *materia musica* into its constituent parts. It was first played at Dumbarton Oaks on 23rd January 1954.

But 'technique' meant 'the whole man'. It was one thing to listen to Webern's music; it was quite another to adopt serial procedures as an integral part of the process of composition; and Stravinsky's adoption of them was gradual, even hesitant. His next piece, *Three songs from William Shakespeare*, for voice and three instruments, was first heard on 8th March the same year, at one of the 'Evenings on the Roof' concerts in Los Angeles. Stravinsky had been associated with these concerts since 1940, and when Craft became his assistant, and also moved to Hollywood in 1949, he conducted several performances there. The concerts reminded Stravinsky of the 'Evenings of Contemporary Music' in old St Petersburg. After September 1954 they gave way to the 'Monday Evening Concerts' under Lawrence Morton. The Shakespeare songs must have put Stravinsky in mind of his earlier essays in song-writing, since he then rescored some of his earlier Russian songs for voice and three instruments (flute, harp and guitar); he also rescored the Balmont songs (1911) for voice and small orchestra.

That year also saw the composition of an *in memoriam* work, the first of several from now on. He had met Dylan Thomas only the previous year, though he had been acquainted with his work since 1950, on Auden's commendation. Now he was enthusiastic to compose an opera on a libretto by Dylan Thomas. The prospect of a commission for such an opera from Boston University, where Stravinsky had just conducted a performance of *The Rake's Progress*, brought the composer and poet together on 22nd May 1953 in Boston, where the idea was discussed. The opera was to represent a re-creation of the world; an atomic disaster would leave only one man and woman alive, and they would experience the whole new awakening to life of aboriginal man.

Stravinsky returned to Hollywood, where he keenly awaited Dylan Thomas's imminent arrival. A special room was even built for him. But the telegram which came on 9th November, which should have announced the time of arrival of his plane, announced his death. It was a bitter moment for Stravinsky. Who can say what the new opera might not have achieved? As it is, the only testament to it is the *In memoriam Dylan Thomas*, for which Stravinsky took the poet's own text 'Do not go gentle into that good night', using tenor and string quartet. This song he preceded and followed with dirge-canons for four trombones, like a cortège.

8 Final fulfilment

Once embarked on what was for him an aesthetically true path, nothing could deflect Stravinsky. In 1935, as he says in the closing pages of the *Chronicles*, he had become aware that the course his composition was taking was losing him the sympathy of former admirers. But this did not cause him to falter in his chosen direction. So now twenty years later, in 1955, his resolve was equally consistent. His career, more than any other composer's, summarizes and consummates the art-music of the twentieth century; for this reason his aesthetic tenets, as shown in his reported conversations and writings as well as in his music, are of almost as much value and concern as his compositions themselves. His creative genius was such that he had always been susceptible to the many facets of new music; he combined intellectual curiosity, and aesthetic sensitivity, with certainty of his own requirements and personality.

His gradual, and personal, assimilation of serialism was pursued in his next work, which was commissioned for the Venice Biennale in 1956. Stravinsky's links with Venice were very close, and several of his works had been performed there; most recently *The Rake's Progress*, which had been such a spectacular success. But the *Canticum Sacrum*, whose purpose and conception were so different, was to be accorded a much less warm reception. The new work, *ad honorem Sancti Marci nominis*, was designed specifically for St Mark's Cathedral, where he conducted the first performance on 13th September 1956. Once again, as in the *Symphony of Psalms*, he achieves a hieratic severity by using only lower strings; but for the first and only time he includes an organ, which was not an instrument he liked. He uses it antiphonally with the other instruments. At the same concert his arrangement of Bach's Choral-Variations 'Vom Himmel hoch' was also played, conducted by Robert Craft.

Stravinsky's itinerary that year was a wide one. Starting in June, it included a tour of Greece and Italy, and took in a visit to Mr and Mrs Bliss on the Bosphorus. After the Venice concert in September he went on to Montreux, Geneva and Berlin. He was ill for a while in Munich, after which he went on to Rome. Next he met his old friend Souvtchinsky in Paris, for the first time since 1939; he returned to California in December. By any standards it was a taxing programme for a man in his seventy-fifth year.

Meanwhile another commission awaited his attention, and one much to his liking, from Lincoln Kirstein and George Balanchine. *Agon* had been started as early as 1954, only to be interrupted by other work, mainly the *Canticum*. He worked on it while in Venice in September 1956. It was his first ballet for ten years; and as they had with *Orpheus*, Stravinsky and Balanchine worked in close co-operation. The stage première took place in New York on 1st December 1957; but Robert Craft conducted it as a concert piece the previous June, at a concert in Los Angeles to mark Stravinsky's seventy-fifth birthday, when it was introduced by Aldous Huxley.

Stravinsky this time chose an abstract subject, without plot; Balanchine in his choreography followed suit. French seventeenth-century Court dances provided the composer with some models; there are also traces of blues and boogie-woogie. Unlike the *Canticum*, the new ballet was well received; *Agon* represents fulfilment in the ballet genre of Stravinsky's particular serial technique in a way that corresponds to the fulfilment that *Movements* was soon to achieve in the orchestral genre.

Stravinsky's conducting schedule for the year of his seventy-fifth birthday included, in January, concerts and recordings in New York and, from August to October, another customary visit to Europe. It was on such a European tour the following year, 1958, that he returned once more to Venice to introduce another sacred choral work during the Biennale programme that year. *Threni* was commissioned by the Norddeutscher Rundfunk of Hamburg, and first played in the Scuola di San Rocco in Venice. This score is one of the most characteristic of the composer's later ones. It contains none of the hesitancy of earlier transitional work, such as the *Canticum*. *Threni* is a sacred work; several more were to follow; but whereas he had hoped that the *Mass* would be used liturgically, he had no such aspiration for *Threni*; which is why it is called not *Tenebrae Service* but *Lamentations*.

Stravinsky next applied his new-found style in an instrumental piece, *Movements* for piano and orchestra. He had not written for such an ensemble since the *Capriccio* thirty years earlier; but now he did not use the piano in a *concertante* role. The use that he made of serial disciplines in his music of these years was to have the effect of concentrating and densifying the musical material in depth. *Movements* is the most characteristic instrumental piece of this style, as *Threni* is among the choral, and *Agon* among the stage works. It was written in 1958–9 and first played in New York on 10th January 1960, with Margrit Weber as soloist, who also commissioned it. The short *Double Canon*, 'Raoul Dufy in Memoriam', was also included in the same programme.

In construction, *Movements* is Stravinsky's most complex score; once again he felt the isolation of creativity. He was to say a few years after this:

While I hardly regret not belonging to a movement, and that the music I now produce answers no commercial and little other demand, I would like to exchange more than a few rapidly crossing glimpses with my colleagues. As it is now, I see eye to eye with no one.

While he wrote with no particular public in mind (he once called them 'the hypothetical other'), and certainly not for any narrow clique or coterie, yet it never occured to him that his music should not be heard by the listener as he intended it should be heard, and as he himself heard it and wrote it. And the same precision governed his aesthetic judgement.

About this time, and largely to forestall the publicity that would inevitably attend his seventy-fifth birthday year (1957), Stravinsky devised with Robert Craft a question-and-answer form of public dialogue. It was almost twenty-five years since the *Chronicles* were published, and these published dialogues would combine autobiography with the composer's views on music in the widest sense. The first attempt had been *Answers to 35 Questions*, published in 1957. This style was later expanded into several books of conversations, the first of which were published in 1959.[1]

The 1960 Biennale again brought Stravinsky to Venice, where on 27th September he conducted his re-composition for orchestra of three madrigals of Gesualdo, under the title *Monumentum pro Gesualdo*. That year marked the four hundredth anniversary of Gesualdo's birth, and Stravinsky had already reconstructed *Tres Cantiones Sacrae*, intending them for performance in 1956 with the *Canticum Sacrum*.

On 15th October, during his stay in Venice, the city was flooded; and this event gave him the title for his next composition, *The Flood*. He had been approached already in 1959 by Robert Graff, for C.B.S. Television, to write a special work for that medium. The title was both actual and symbolic; it stood for a contemporarary image of catastrophe, the atomic bomb, rather than merely the historical Noah. He discussed the idea with T. S. Eliot, whose suggestion of the 'universality' of the Noah story impressed him. Moreover, the theme of Dylan

[1] See Appendix D—Bibliography.

Thomas's libretto was to have been a kindred one, rebirth after a cosmic disaster.

As it happened, *The Flood* was to be the last of Stravinsky's dramatic works—that chain of eighteen major compositions spanning a period of more than fifty years, from *The Firebird* to *The Flood*, each one breaking new ground, none duplicating the others. Perhaps appropriately, it appeared to Gunther Rennert, who directed the stage production at Hamburg in 1963, that *The Flood* was a sort of résumé of Stravinsky's different theatrical forms—opera, ballet, narration, pantomime. Such a stratification, triggered off by the cinematic effects of television, is the visual and theatrical equivalent of the many layers of his serial style. The text was chosen and arranged by Robert Craft, principally from Genesis, and from the York and Chester miracle plays. The scenario is complicated, and the subject is not the Noah story as such, but sin. Whereas the music of *Petrushka* was representational, the music of *The Flood* is symbolic.

Television seemed to Stravinsky to offer every advantage over stage opera; but what chiefly interested him, characteristically, was the 'saving of musical time'. Visual effect is instantaneous; the composer therefore can dispense with 'connecting' music—overtures, entr'actes—and the speed of Stravinsky's music for *The Flood* is so conceived cinematographically that he could not at first imagine a stage production. The work was written in 1961 and finished in March the following year, after which he worked on the details of the television production with Balanchine and Craft. It was screened on 14th June. That year also saw another important première, on 23rd February, when a new cantata, written for Paul Sacher and the Basler Kammerorchester was first heard in Basel. *A Sermon, a Narrative and a Prayer* stands directly in line with *Threni*, except that its text is drawn from the New Testament, not the Old.

Meanwhile Stravinsky, the inveterate traveller, continued to extend the range of his visits. In 1961, in addition to his customary visit to Europe, his itinerary also took in Egypt, Australia, New Zealand and Tahiti. Moreover in June he received a visit from a group of Russian composers, including Khrennikov, who officially invited him to visit the Soviet Union the following year, the occasion of his eightieth birthday. Nothing could have been more unexpected, more controversial, or more deeply welcome to Stravinsky. He discussed the prospect with a fellow émigré, Vladimir Ussachevsky. His lack of respect for the Soviet treatment of composers was well known, and had been amply repaid by abuse in the official Soviet press; but he finally decided to accept, as he said, for the sake of the younger Russian musicians, with whom he was only too ready to make contact.

The year 1962 indeed began auspiciously with concerts and recordings. Then on 18th January he and Vera were entertained to dinner at the White House by President and Mrs Kennedy. Stravinsky's subsequent travels that year took him all over the world—to France, South Africa, Italy, Germany—where he celebrated his eightieth birthday on 18th June with a concert in Hamburg; then after returning to America, for concerts in New York, Chicago and Hollywood, he set out again on 21st August on what was to be the climactic journey of his life, taking him to Israel, Venice, Paris—and finally Moscow. It was on 21st September that he returned to his native Russia, after forty-eight years' absence. He was greeted with concerts, receptions, sightseeing. Among the welcoming committee at the city now called Leningrad was one elderly man, who addressed him formally as 'Igor Fedorovich', but whom Stravinsky failed to recognize; partly because the last time they met in 1910 he had been called 'Guima', which was the name by which he was known in his youth among his close friends. It was Vladimir Rimsky-Korsakov. Everywhere he went Stravinsky was acclaimed. It was the most moving experience of his life.

9 Envoi

Stravinsky's visit to Israel in the summer of 1962 gave him the inspiration, and the occasion, for another vocal work, *Abraham and Isaac*. He was asked by the Committee of the Festival of Israel (1964) to compose a new work for them; he began the new 'Sacred Ballad' without delay, and worked on it during the remainder of his tour that year to Russia. It was finished by March 1963, in time for him to leave on a concert tour of Europe the following month. This included the staging of *The Flood* in Hamburg on 30th April, and a performance by Monteux in London of *Le Sacre du printemps* on 29th May—the fiftieth anniversary of the notorious première. Unfortunately it was a poor performance.

The year 1963 was overshadowed for the composer, as it was for countless other Americans and Europeans, by the assassination of President Kennedy on 22nd November. Stravinsky heard the news in a hotel in Catania, while on a tour which took him to Sicily and Italy; indeed his last concert in Rome on 25th November coincided with the day of the American President's funeral. This occasion was made doubly painful by the death, also on 22nd November, of his close friend Aldous Huxley. Both these bereavements, the one personal, the other international, were recorded with *in memoriam* works. He had already embarked on the orchestral *Variations*, which were begun in Santa Fé in July, and he decided to dedicate them to the memory of Aldous Huxley. They continue his development of serialism from the point where *Movements* left off.

The other *in memoriam* piece, the *Elegy for J.F.K.*, which was first heard on 6th April 1964, at one of the 'Monday Evening Concerts' in Los Angeles, is short and very different. Stravinsky asked W. H. Auden for a 'very quiet little lyric', which he then set for baritone and three clarinets. An event of such magnitude as the President's murder might, in many, lead to epic sentiments of symphonic proportions. But Auden's elegy, in the form of a *haiku*, sparked off in Stravinsky a figure of just two reiterated notes, which he calls a 'melodic rhythmic stutter', frequently used in numerous works from *Les Noces* to the *Concerto in D*. Once he had completed the vocal part, the instrumental counterpoint fell naturally into place.

That year began and ended for Stravinsky with concerts in America; but the highlight was without doubt his visit to Jerusalem in August for the first performance there, during the Festival of Israel, of *Abraham and Isaac*. Following *The Flood*, he again set a section of Genesis, this time in Hebrew, which he discussed with Isaiah Berlin; as usual, though he worked with the English version as well, it was the sound of the new language that attracted him. Once again, as in the case of *Threni*, his serial technique led him to discover a fresh sort of tonality. He himself rated the work highly.

It was inevitable that his pronounced leaning towards religious works at this time, coupled with the number of *in memoriam* pieces, would lead him sooner or later to write a Requiem. But the death of T. S. Eliot on 4th January 1965 first caused him to write the short *Introitus*, a setting for male-voice choir and eight instruments of the opening words of the Latin Requiem: 'Requiem aeternam dona ei, Domine, et lux perpetua luceat ei'. It was finished on 17th February that year, and first heard in Chicago two months later, on 17th April, together with the *Variations*. The following month he visited Poland, the country of origin of his family, for the first time for forty years; but he was unable to see Oustilug. A subsequent visit to Italy culminated in his being decorated by Pope Paul at a concert in the Vatican.

The year 1965 saw the beginning of what was to prove his last substantial composition. The form of the *Requiem Canticles* 'is that of a *retablo* of small panels rather than a large-scale fresco'; fragments of the text are interlarded with instrumental music. Stravinsky looked on the work as 'a monument ordered, like Mozart's, by a mysterious stranger'. He seems to have had a foreboding that it would be his own Requiem; 'for Venice' were his words later. He finished the work on 13th August 1966, and Robert Craft directed the first performance at Princeton on 8th October. The *Requiem Canticles* for contralto and bass soli, chorus and orchestra, are Stravinsky's last substantial composition; but they are not his last composition. As he said while writing it, 'I will be mightily relieved to be done with it and to get on to something else.'

The 'something else' was a short song for voice and piano; a personal piece, dedicated simply 'to Vera'. *The Owl and the Pussy Cat* was written between August and October that year. It was characteristic of the composer, both that he should thus turn to his wife, who had been his constant companion and ally for some fifty years, and that in so doing he should revert to his earliest form of composition. According to Craft, *The Owl and the Pussy Cat* was the first English verse that Vera committed to memory. Later she became almost as fond of Francis Steeg-muller's French version of it, and it was the latter that originally attracted Stravinsky to the poem. Its first performance took place in Hollywood at one of Lawrence Morton's 'Monday Evening Concerts', on Halloween, 1966.

Stravinsky's conducting schedule for 1966 was as busy as ever, including appearances all over the United States, and in May a tour of Paris, Athens and Lisbon, where on 1st June he conducted *Oedipus Rex*. It was in the midst of conducting engagements that the *Requiem Canticles* was written; his 'pocket

Requiem', as he called it, because most of it was composed in notebooks which he carried with him. But he was now in his eighty-fifth year, and clearly he would soon have to reduce the amount of concert-work he undertook. Indeed the following year, 1967, marked his last appearances as conductor of his own works. In January he conducted his final recording in Chicago, when he directed that same work with which his conducting career had opened at Diaghilev's instigation over fifty years previously, in December 1915—*The Firebird*. In March he conducted *Histoire du soldat* in Seattle; then what proved to be his last concert was given in Toronto, where on 17th May he conducted *Pulcinella*. For the first and last time in his conducting career, he remained seated.

During the later part of August that year he was in hospital, returning home to convalesce early in September. His friends found his intellectual vigour and extraordinary powers of observation quite undiminished. George Balanchine called, discussing, as usual, new choreographic ideas; Pierre Souvtchinsky came over from Paris, on Robert Craft's suggestion, and listened to *Les Noces* and the *Requiem Canticles*—the old and the new aspects of Stravinsky's choral output. He had some penetrating comments to make about the composer's Russian background, and the 'Diaghilev myth'.

Was the composer's life nearing its close? Was this the time to draw the threads together of his extraordinarily rich and long-lasting output? His return to hospital in November made it seem so; but by the end of the year he had made a remarkable recovery. On 25th December he came to the dinner-table, walking with the aid of a nurse; first, he pointed out, because it was Vera's birthday; second, because it was Christmas—in that order.

The following year saw something of a resumption of the normal pattern of his life. He had begun to compose some piano pieces in December 1966; now he abandoned these, and in

January 1968 he had in mind a bigger piece. In May he orchestrated two songs from Hugo Wolf's *Spanisches Liederbuch* for Marilyn Horne, which were sung in September. His itinerary that year took him in the early part of the year to concerts in Oakland, Phoenix, Los Angeles and San Francisco; but he found the strain heavier than before. Between September and November he was in Europe, staying in Zürich at Paul Sacher's invitation, and in Paris, where on 8th November he heard *Le Sacre* at the Opéra.

At this time the two closest to him, his wife Vera and Robert Craft, considered the question of moving residence from California, where he had lived since 1940. Paris was suggested. But when the change was eventually made, in September 1969, it was to New York, largely for medical reasons. On 27th April 1969 he attended a concert of his music at Stony Brook, Long Island; but five days later he was taken to hospital in New York, where he underwent an operation. After his discharge (on his birthday, 18th June) he returned to Hollywood; then on 14th September he left California permanently and moved to New York, to the Essex House.

During the last few years of his life he was not able to complete any further compositions satisfactorily. His creative will was still there, however, and he made several beginnings; indeed one month before he died he began a new composition with an 'idea beginning with combinations of *tierces*'. But for the most part he transcribed—particularly some of Bach's preludes and fugues from the *Well-tempered Clavier*. These were scheduled by Nicholas Nabokov for performance on 2nd October 1969 at the Berlin Festival; but in the event he and Craft decided that they were not suitable for performance under Stravinsky's name as they stood.

His greatest pleasure at this time came from listening to music on records. Robert Craft would arrange evenings of recorded music, particularly the late Beethoven quartets. Attending concerts, and hearing music, had been Stravinsky's life since boyhood; now in his old age this could only be through records. He was in hospital again at Lenox Hill in April 1970, but recovered enough to pay his last visit to Europe that summer. He stayed at Evian. In December that year Vera bought a new apartment in New York, but the composer was not to see it for more than a few days. After another illness in hospital in March 1971 he and his wife left the Essex House on 30th March and moved to the new apartment. It was there that his last illness began on 4th April. He died in the early morning of 6th April, the Tuesday of Holy Week.

The first, private, funeral ceremony took place on Good Friday. The following Monday the composer's body was flown to Rome, then to Venice, for the public funeral and interment on 15th April. The previous day the coffin was placed in the Cappella del Rosario, in the church of S.S. Giovanni e Paolo, where the Mass for the dead was to be conducted. The music included the *Requiem Canticles*. Then the bier was borne by gondola to the island of San Michele, where the burial took place, in a grave near that of Diaghilev.

Interlude

And now, what is the nature of the work, and the significance, of this remarkable composer, without whose monumental achievement the story of twentieth-century Western music would be unthinkable? Whatever the period of his threefold career, Russian, neo-classical or serial, and whatever the influences and models he might adopt, the music of Stravinsky contains an irreducible core that is identifiably his alone. Born as he was outside the Austro-German tradition, he was therefore not subject to it. Rather it aroused his curiosity, which he exercised eclectically—the more so after about 1920, when his first Russian period was past. He came to Bach and Beethoven comparatively late; thereafter as the years passed, and neoclassicism gave way to serialism, his musical models were taken from earlier periods and included the mediaeval and Renaissance composers. He took whatever whetted his musical appetite, transformed it and made it his own.

And what of the character and personality of this man, that gave him the vision and tenacity to steer a course through the maelstrom of contemporary music, and thereby to transcend its self-imposed decadence and decay?

He was a man to whom true friendship was of great importance; though about untrue friendship, as about bad music, he could be quite ruthless and caustic. At every stage of his life he made, and retained, numerous friendships; for the most part among creative artists in many fields of activity: writers, painters, poets, philosophers, dancers, as well as musicians. Mitusov,

Rimsky-Korsakov,Diaghilev;Souvtchinsky,Nijinsky,Ansermet, Picasso, Ramuz, Cingria, Cocteau; Huxley, Auden, Isherwood, Balanchine, Nabokov, Craft. Thus his art was the very opposite of isolated and élitist. It became, on the contrary, broad and suffused with warmth.

He was a man of unshakeable religious faith. Catholic culture, in the widest sense, imbues his work, particularly after the *Symphony of Psalms*. As an adolescent he criticized the rites and feasts of the Orthodox Church, which had been strictly observed by the Stravinsky family since childhood; and it was not until 1926 that he re-entered the Russian Church. Slavonic was, for him, the 'language of prayer'. The *Pater noster* was written that year to mark the event.

He was a man whose intellectual energy rested on a central fact—the creative importance of language; the power of words, whether as units of thought or as the means of communication. He was multilingual, and reverted to Russian in the last years of his life. When he moved to France after the First World War, what caused him the greatest problem artistically was the abandonment of the Russian language, which he had used for nearly forty years, and the consequent search for another, which he might call his own.

Finally he was a man of order; that wider search for order in his compositions was reflected at every level of his day-to-day life, down to the fanatical tidiness of his workroom. Disorder, whether social or musical, was anathema to him, a fact to which numerous of his contemporaries have testified—Tansman, Nabokov, Dushkin. For this reason, too, his concern for his health amounted almost to hypochondria. This may well have originated from his frail health in childhood, to say nothing of the death of so many of his nearest family from tuberculosis. He was a man who permitted nothing, as far as lay within him, to obstruct the flow of his creativity—which, well into his eighties, continued unabatedly to alter the face of Western music.

10 Stage works (I)

BALLETS

It was with *The Firebird* that Stravinsky suddenly, abruptly, achieved international acclaim; and although this was by no means his first orchestral score, he was as yet unproved as a composer. He turned away from merely descriptive music—the iridescence of Rimsky-Korsakov's aesthetic, the impressionism of Debussy's; instead he delighted in his own discovery of orchestral effects—trombone *glissandi*, *glissandi* for strings using natural harmonics, his own violence and primitivism; and though traces can be shown of Tchaikovsky and Rimsky-Korsakov, of the influence of a Mendelssohnian scherzo, and the quotation of Russian folk melodies,[1] the overall effect is one of glitter, sparkle and brilliance; of extremes of contrast; of orchestral virtuosity.

Indeed the very popular success of *The Firebird* was to prove, ironically enough, something of an obstacle to the acceptance of some of his later scores. The audiences who applauded this work were not at all anxious, subsequently, to follow its creator into fresh, more original, uncharted territories; it was for this score that he became chiefly known, whether in the theatre, where it gained approval, even in Soviet Russia, or in the concert hall, for which he later wrote two revised versions, in 1919 and 1945, trimming and economizing what he saw as an excessively long

[1] The two 'Khorovod' themes ('Ronde des Princesses') and the finale theme.

original score into a six-movement suite; it was even his later view that the concert suite made a better ballet-score than the original version.

With his next ballet, *Petrushka,* he further established his individualism. By following the dictates of none but himself, and his own ear, he marked more clearly the rift with 'The Five'. The score is more individual, more original, than *The Firebird,* and he had a more direct hand in the details of scene and character than in the previous work. He had the clearest idea of his characters; the Charlatan was conceived as one out of Hoffmann, the Moor as a Wilhelm Busch caricature; as for Petrushka himself, his ghost is the real one; previously he is a mere doll, a pathetic figure in baggy clothes. The fairground set was an open piazza, such as the Champs de Mars in St Petersburg, where the Mardi Gras Carnival used to take place.

Stravinsky was particularly pleased with the ending of the score, both dramatically and musically, and with Petrushka's ghostly resurrection—which was his idea, not that of Benois. Moreover, the bitonal music of the second tableau,[1] which represents Petrushka's insult to the public, recurs at the close,[2] to show that his ghost is still behaving in the same way. Something of the ending of *Petrushka* was later recalled by Berg in the ending of the *March,* No. 3 of his *Three Orchestral Pieces* (1914), in which a climax is followed by the quiet of solo instruments. In Stravinsky's case the ending of *Petrushka* was the first intimation of an important structural discovery: that final apotheosis, which is a marked feature of many later works.

The world of *Petrushka,* the Russian Punch and Judy, appealed equally strongly to Stravinsky and to Benois, and they revelled in it. Most of the impetuous score is at a fast tempo, as one dance succeeds another; what slow passages there are, such

---

[1] At figs. 95, 118.
[2] At fig. 267—2.

as the flute cadenza of the Showman,[1] or Petrushka's music in the second tableau, represent pauses before the next outburst. Against the background of the Shrove-tide fair, Stravinsky enacts his drama through the music itself. The first and fourth tableaux take place at the Carnival, while the middle two tableaux concern the more intimate world of the dolls, who have come to life in the first tableau. Thus reality and the world of dreams fuse together. Petrushka represents striving, oppressed, suffering humanity; the Ballerina represents the eternal feminine, that elusive goal towards which men strive; the Moor represents selfish ambition, worldly, unprincipled, yet triumphant—against which Petrushka is powerless.

Petrushka presents Russian peasant revelry, gypsies, masqueraders (*riageni*), and all the drunken bustle of the St Petersburg Carnival. As well as characteristic melodic material, of the sort that occurs frequently in Stravinsky's work from now on, the score also contains some metrical innovation, and novelties of scoring, which are a direct foretaste of his next and most notorious ballet-score.

If we appreciate *Petrushka* chiefly as a piece of theatre, of which the score is the brilliantly apt musical extension, we appreciate *Le Sacre* chiefly as a piece of abstract music, conceived on a totally different æsthetic basis. Whereas discussion of the first ranges over the characters and background as well as the music itself, discussion of the second naturally focuses on Stravinsky's technical discoveries; and the background-theme of the ballet (the young sacrificial virgin dancing herself to death; the wise elders propitiating the tribal god) is comparatively less important.

In *Le Sacre* Stravinsky brings rhythm to the fore as a constituent structural element. The rhythmic development imposes an architectural form on each section; new forms are the result.

[1] Fig. 60.

In this respect he was reverting to the practices of the Middle Ages, when rhythm was treated on an equality with other musical elements; isorhythm was one way used by the mediaeval composers to avoid formlessness—and indeed later, after 1950, Stravinsky was particularly susceptible to the movement which sought to recapture the methods and techniques of pre-Classical composers, particularly as far as rhythm was concerned, which had been lost sight of in Western music since the eighteenth-century establishment of harmony as the primary musical element.

His scheme is strict. Periods are made up of equal and unequal rhythms; there is thus just as much a contrast between the rhythms making up a theme as there is between the themes making up a section, and between the sections throughout the work. The repose of the Introduction is broken by *Les Augures printaniers*; the *presto* of the *Jeu du rapt* is followed by the *sostenuto* of *Rondes printanières*. The first part, *L'Adoration de la terre*, ends *prestissimo* with the *Danse de la terre*; the second part, *Le Sacrifice*, begins ponderously and solemnly with an *Introduction* and *Cercles mystérieux*. An equal, simple pulsation is then replaced by the unequal, complex rhythm of *Glorification de l'élue*. This scheme is then repeated; the simple crotchet beat of *Évocation des ancêtres* and *Action rituelle des ancêtres* leads to the rhythmic complexities of the final, climactic *Danse sacrale*.

Rhythmic subtlety is achieved in two principal ways; first by the addition of an extra pulse-unit to make an irregular pattern; second by the juxtaposition of different patterns to make an unequal rhythmic phrase:

Ex. 1
(a) *Danse Sacrale*

(b) *Cercles mystérieux des Adolescentes*

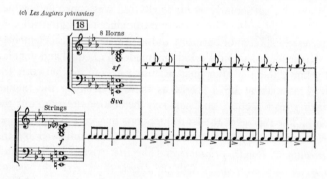

(c) *Les Augures printaniers*

Rhythmic cells are used to build structures in a way corresponding to the use of motivic cells by the Viennese classical composers. This is particularly well shown in the final rondo, the *Danse Sacrale*.[1] Melodic material is mainly diatonic, though disguised with chromaticism and repeated chords. Harmonically *Le Sacre* is a direct continuation of *Petrushka*. In this way nothing is allowed to stand in the way of the exploitation of rhythm, which is also underlined by the instrumental texture. Thus the episodes, musically unrelated, establish their own identity with strict control. Moreover Stravinsky's incisive rhythms are a direct invitation to the choreographer.

The gigantic achievement of *Le Sacre*, which was to prove central to his entire output, marked the end of a phase for Stravinsky. His next production for Diaghilev was the opera *Le Rossignol*, which may be considered separately. After this he

[1] See the Messiaen-Boulez analysis in Boulez's *Relevés d'apprenti*.

reverted to two small-theatre works. For the first of these, instead of the mysteries of pagan Russia, he chose a burlesque tale of four animals; instead of the huge orchestra that Diaghilev had made available for *Le Sacre*, he preferred the more intimate sound of chamber music. *Renard* is a cantata with mime, enacted, like the other small-theatre work *Histoire du soldat*, in the style of a mediaeval morality play. Afanasiev's story gave scope for real satire—the fox disguised as a nun, whose music [1] is a quasi-plainchant; the delicate *guzla*, like a balalaika, whose sound is imitated by the cimbalom in Stravinsky's orchestra, played by the clumsy, cloven-hoofed goat; the cock twice seduced.

Musically it is a continuation of the style of song-writing that occupied his attention between 1913 and 1917. For instance, the reiteration of '*Tiouc, tiouc*',[2] with a characteristic orchestral chord, built round the cimbalom, is very similar to the reiteration of '*Tilimbom*'. Such songs as the *Trois histoires*, the *Berceuses du chat*, and particularly the nonsense-words of the *Pribaoutki*, had led Stravinsky to a vocal style of syllabic accentuation, difficult to achieve in any language other than Russian. In *Renard* the metres are mechanical, and for the first time are built round related metronome values.

The four male singers, placed with the orchestra, are treated orchestrally, and their function is to describe the action. They are not directly identified with the four animals, whose parts are enacted on the stage in mime by four dancing acrobats.

The second small-theatre work, the allegorical *Histoire du soldat*, is more rhythmically concentrated than *Renard*, and the music is broken up into short sections, allowing it to be played separately as an instrumental suite. The jazz element is more pronounced than in *Renard*, both in the instrumentation and the treatment of the material. Stravinsky had not heard any jazz in 1918; he had merely seen the ragtime scores that Ansermet

---

[1] At fig. 12.   [2] Beginning at fig. 62.

brought from America—and had reinterpreted them as he saw fit. When in 1919 he heard a live band he quickly realized that the essential improvisatory element of jazz makes the performance much more interesting than the composition of it. Its influence on his work thereafter was short-lived.

The movements of *Histoire du soldat* use related material; for instance the trombone theme that opens the *Royal March* recurs later in the *Chorale*; the four-note bass *ostinato* that begins the music for the soldier at the brook (Scene 1) is used again later in the *Devil's Dance*, at fig. 4.

Histoire du soldat continues the exploitation of the elements of music, particularly metre, rhythm and tonality, where *Le Sacre*, and *Les Noces*, left off. It breaks new ground, if only because greater subtlety and intricacy of rhythmic invention is possible with a small group of musicians than with a large one. The addition of small pulse-units to, or their subtraction from, the regular and expected phrase-shape leads to delayed or anticipated accentuation, or syncopation against the beat, or to the clash of contrasted rhythmic patterns. Stravinsky also achieved a new expressive dimension by superimposing varied rhythmic patterns over a constant, basic metre; by varying the metre but not the pulse-unit, or metrical *ostinato*; by introducing two or more metres simultaneously. Examples occur in the opening *Soldier's March*, and the *Little Concert* at fig. 21. The same principle was used much later in *Agon*, where a metrical *ostinato* is provided by a castanet in the *Bransle Gay*.

Apart from its technical advances, *Histoire du soldat* is unique for other reasons. It is the only one of Stravinsky's theatre works to have a contemporary theme; it is also the only work in which one of the motifs was written down from a dream, although several works originated in dreams—*Le Sacre*, for instance, and the *Octet*; but in the case of *Histoire du soldat* he saw a young gypsy playing the violin, and this became the material for the *Little Concert*. Although in Stravinsky's case the

use of a small number of instruments was dictated by the requirements of a travelling troupe, there were recent precedents for
such an ensemble in Schoenberg's *Pierrot Lunaire* (1912), and
Ravel's *Trois Poèmes de Stéphane Mallarmé* (1913), as well as
his own *Japanese Lyrics*. Moreover, though *Histoire du soldat*,
like *Renard*, was partly the result of the exigencies of war time,
it marked the final stage of Stravinsky's break from the Russian
orchestral school. He had emancipated himself from one tradition, and had not yet bound himself to another; and from now
on he began to glance at other past periods of music with peculiar
interest and concern.

The first such glance led to the very next ballet, *Pulcinella*.
The resumption of work with Diaghilev, after the war, and his
collaboration with Massine and Picasso, was a happy experience
for the composer. Pulcinella was the traditional hero of Neapolitan *commedia dell'arte*; and the plot, which is concerned with
his amorous adventures, is a disguise comedy, simple to the
point of ridicule. But if Diaghilev expected a strict orchestration
of Pergolesi's music, mannered according to the eighteenth-
century style, he was to be disappointed.

Stravinsky's chief sources were two of Pergolesi's operas, *Il
Fratello Innamorato* (1732) and *Il Flaminio* (1735), as well as trio
sonatas and other pieces. To these melodies of Pergolesi
Stravinsky brought his own scoring, with characteristic
instrumental groupings, and individual effects, such as string
harmonics and trombone *glissandi*; once again singers are placed
in the orchestra, as in *Renard*. The period generally called
'neoclassicism' had begun.

In contrast to eighteenth-century Italy, *Les Noces* presents
the very different world of a traditional Russian peasant wedding.
Of all Stravinsky's ballets it is the most typically and specifically
Russian; Diaghilev certainly thought so, which is the reason
for the dedication to him. It dates from the early war years, which
was a period of exploration and discovery, and was finished in

79

short score by 1917, before *Histoire du soldat*. Indeed the idea of such dance scenes came to Stravinsky as early as 1912, while finishing *Le Sacre*. The dance-cantata form was suggested by the material in Kireievsky's anthology, from which the composer took his libretto. The words are typical wedding clichés, with ritualistic undertones, and invocations to the Virgin, as well as to various fertility deities.

The percussive material, matched by the highly unusual instrumentation for four pianos and percussion, is written in additive rhythms, which are conceived horizontally with constantly variable metres; not in polyrhythm, which is conceived vertically. The limited scope of melodic material influenced by folk music, as in *Le Sacre*, further draws attention to the mechanical, relentless nature of its treatment. Overriding the changes of metre, the metrical unit remains strict, and it is this unvarying pulse which gives the music its energy, and the dances their vitality. Stravinsky visualized the players and singers together on stage.

No characters stand out; even the bride and bridegroom are to some extent puppets, enacting a traditional rite; so the choreography should be in blocks, and avoid stressing individual personalities. The set can also be visually empty; the music itself makes its own necessary changes of scene. The voices carry the work throughout, and the instruments do not play a single bar by themselves, until the final curtain-coda. The vocal style continues that of *Renard* or *Pribaoutki*; the metre follows that of the text, while the melodic material makes plentiful use of repeated notes, within a limited compass.

OPERAS

Stravinsky disliked many aspects of opera. He was disenchanted with the aesthetic basis on which, since Wagner, it rested. 'Music-drama' was an idea to which he was antipathetic, while the con-

ception of 'endless melody' was for him a contradiction in terms.
So the composition of opera presented aesthetic problems to
him which did not exist in the case of ballet. The path to the
discovery of a new classicism appropriate to ballet was unim-
peded; but classicism in opera had been practically obliterated
by the 'inflated arrogance' of the Wagnerian conception of
'music-drama', which represented no tradition and fulfilled no
musical necessity. The operas of Stravinsky's maturity, particularly *Mavra* and *The Rake's Progress*, may be seen as his
solutions of this problem.

His first opera, *Le Rossignol*, which he calls a 'lyric tale',
stands midway between opera and ballet, with a marked leaning
to the latter. It seeks a solution of the opera problem along
Debussy's path of 'lyric-drama'; alone of his operas it was
capable of being adapted into a symphonic poem for concert
use, with the minimum of alteration. It was concerned not with
action or character, but with a story; and a disembodied, tongue-
in-cheek fairy-story at that. It was also a spectacle, sumptuous
and impressive, the last to be staged by Diaghilev before Europe
was plunged, two months later, into war.

The chief moment of this stage-spectacular is the Emperor
of China's march, which so affected Benois that for the first
time in his life he felt genuinely moved by one of his own
creations. Stravinsky had the model before him of the coronation
scene in Mussorgsky's *Boris*; while as for the love of things
Oriental, this was something that was equally strongly felt in
Paris and St Petersburg at this time.

Mavra is more of an opera than *Le Rossignol*, and has clean,
formal divisions into solos, duets, ensembles. It is a one-act
opera buffa, a charming take-off of the *romances sentimentales*
of nineteenth-century Russian composers, built round a Russo-
Italian melodic line. The music stays within the hundred-years-
old tradition of Glinka and Dargomijsky; not in an attempt to
re-establish that tradition, but to realize the form of *opéra-bouffe*,

which was so well suited to the subject; that dialogue-in-music whose style had been lost. The plot tells of a hussar who dresses up as a cook (Mavra) to obtain admission into the household of his betrothed (Parasha), only to be discovered shaving by Parasha's mother and a neighbour. The joke contained in Kochno's libretto, based on the Pushkin story *The little house in Kolomna,* is well matched by the wit contained in Stravinsky's music— that on to the long melodic lines of *bel canto*, with frequent repetition of words and phrases, the composer has grafted his recently minted metrical discoveries.

The score thus has a freshness, a subtlety, which the nineteenth-century period and the Italian influence cannot conceal, only offset. In this respect, although the joke fell distinctly flat at the first performance, the opera marks a turning point in Stravinsky's thought. Its stylistic successor, though not for thirty years, was *The Rake's Progress.*

11 Stage works (II)

All Stravinsky's stage works differ. Each represents a fresh solution to the ever-present problem of relating music within a chosen framework of drama, whether sung, spoken, danced or mimed. Words, action, choreography, set, all contrive to distract attention from the music. Stravinsky's solutions varied; he might introduce words without action, as in *Oedipus Rex*; or action without words, as in *Orpheus*; or words with action, or with choreography. *Persephone* combines them all. The only element common to all the stage works is the primacy of the music.

In *Oedipus Rex* the events themselves are concentrated into the music, and the only stage-movements are entrances and exits; moreover the moving characters (Speaker, Tiresias, Messenger, Shepherd) are secondary figures; the agents of Destiny, not its victims. Nothing could afford a greater contrast to the light-weight, charming, satirical *Mavra*.

Oedipus Rex is static, monumental, archetypal drama. Just as Greek tragedy was itself a compound of drama, history and myth, with the action taking place off-stage, so Stravinsky's work is part profane (opera), part sacred (oratorio). With the chorus stretched across the stage, the singers appear like statues; at different heights, in masks which restrict their movements. These, combined with the narrator in evening dress and the use of a dead language, Latin, combine to hold the audience at a distance, and to portray nervous energy and mystery; indeed the themes of etachment and alienation are Brechtian concepts.

The music too has a monumental quality, and is tonally and harmonically simple. Unlike earlier works, the rhythm is more static and regular and follows the rhythms of Sophocles'choruses; unlike Stravinsky's earlier vocal style, accentuation is decided by musical, not linguistic, considerations. The second syllable of Oedipus is a case in point. The word 'oracula' also gives rise to an insistent rhythmic pattern. A minor tonality predominates, gradually dropping, but offset by the occasional section in the major, such as Creon's air at fig. 25, or the sudden outburst at fig. 90; and the harmony and orchestral sonority are built up from the bass line, as Handel would have done. The texture has a firmness, a classical solidity, for this reason. There is also a strong Verdi influence, particularly in the use of the chorus.

The idea of deriving rhythms from Sophocles' verse led to the 'versification' theme of the next ballet, *Apollo*. Here Stravinsky chose not a tragic sequence of grand proportions, culminating in a dire climax; indeed not a dramatic story of any kind, but a single idea or episode, as the Muses show Apollo their arts for his approval, before he leads them away to Parnassus.

The basic rhythm is the Greek iambic, of which the individual dances are variations, or musical Alexandrines. The material, though simply diatonic, and the sonority, though solely for strings, are nevertheless characteristic of Stravinsky—the variation of phrase-length, the occasional metrical experiment, the final apotheosis. Just as *Pulcinella* was a glance back to eighteenth-century Italy, so *Apollo* was a glance back to seventeenth-century France—the static style of Lully, the sets containing the emblems of Le Roi Soleil, with chariot, horses, sun. Other models suggested are Delibes, Debussy, even Saint-Saëns. Stravinsky's concern for pure, abstract, white ballet led to this score, which is the most 'controlled, limited and worked upon' of all his ballets; the chief example of intellect holding sway over expression. This aspect of Stravinsky's work, which extended from *Apollo* to *The Rake's Progress*, found no understanding from the later *avant-garde* of the 1950s and 60s, who regarded it as a 'retrograde' and 'irrelevant' aesthetic choice.

There followed an interlude. *Le Baiser de la fée*, if not complete Stravinsky, represents important facets of his attitude: his affinity with the tradition that Tchaikovsky represented, and his projection of Tchaikovsky's method, which was to frame the classical dance like a ritual drama. There were two important differences between this work of transcription and *Pulcinella*; this was an act of homage, since he belonged to the tradition of Tchaikovsky, not to that of Pergolesi; moreover he knew Tchaikovsky's work intimately, particularly since the *Sleeping Beauty* production of 1921, whereas Pergolesi's work was unknown to him before *Pulcinella*. The sources he selected for *Le Baiser de la fée* were Tchaikovsky's piano pieces and songs, not the orchestral works; he thus allowed for his own characteristic orchestration and use of instruments.

After the interlude of *Le Baiser de la fée*, Stravinsky resumed his original work, with another ballet on a subject of classical mythology. *Persephone*, a 'melodrama in three tableaux', uses music in the context of all other dramatic possibilities—speech, solo and choral song, mime and dance. Its subject material is nearer to *Apollo* than to *Oedipus Rex*; that is to say, it deals not with dramatic events, and their consequences, but with a single, mythological situation.

Persephone, daughter of Demeter, goddess of fertility, plucks the forbidden narcissus, whereupon she is filled with compassion for the Shades of the Underworld, and descends to them. She reigns over them, and during this time winter grips the earth, until her return in the spring. The theme is thus one of tenderness and compassion, in distinction to that of *Oedipus*, which is sterner. The music, too, is correspondingly more delicate, motionless, feminine in timbre.

Stravinsky treated French as he had treated Latin in *Oedipus*, and Russian before that; the stresses were musical and rhythmic, not verbal. Gide had provided 'une structure syllabique excellente', which, so it seemed to Stravinsky, awaited the temporal and rhythmical organization of the music. Gide did not accept such a view; nor did many others; and so to meet this criticism Stravinsky set out his views in a manifesto.[1] His words provide chapter and verse for the aesthetic grounds on which he rested his case for the autonomy of music in stage compositions, from which nothing is allowed to detract.

Brilliance and wit are the chief characteristics of the next ballet-score, *Jeu de cartes*. It might be subtitled 'The Joker's Merry Pranks'; the music contains echoes of *Capriccio* (to say nothing of a satirical quotation from Rossini's *Barber of Seville* at fig. 153). Baulked of Cocteau's collaboration, Stravinsky set about the task of writing the libretto himself. He had the clearest picture in his mind, with the stages of play (deal, passes, bets and so on) allotted dances according to the normal ways of ballet. At the end of each deal a giant croupier's fingers remove the rejected cards, while the dances themselves are a series of doubled *fouettés,* and *brisés* accelerated or retarded; no pirouettes, and nothing to detract from the simplicity of a one-dimensional, 'card-like' ballet.

After *Danses Concertantes* and *Scènes de Ballet,* which were instrumental compositions conceived abstractly apart from the stage, the next ballet as such again took Stravinsky back to a classical theme. Like *Persephone*, the story of *Orpheus* is concerned with the Underworld; and the music too recalls the gloom of Tartarus. Unlike *Persephone*, this work has a savage, dramatic climax, as the Bacchantes attack Orpheus and tear him to pieces. But this is the only moment of violence in the whole ballet; elsewhere the music is restrained, and even the music for the

[1] On 1st May 1934 (quoted in White, op. cit., p. 533).

Stravinsky with his four children. Clarens, 1915

Hollywood, 1944

With Claudio Arrau (*L*) and Joseph Szigeti (*R*). New York, 1946

With Robert Craft (*R*) and Franco Autori (*L*). New York, 1953

With George Balanchine, rehearsing *Agon* for the first performance
with the New York City Ballet, 1957

At a recording session, 1960

Hollywood, 1964

With Derrik Olsen, Lina Lalandi, after conducting *Oedipus Rex*. Athens, 1966

Furies in the second scene, though *agitato*, is on a soft dynamic level.

If *Jeu de cartes* is a continuation of the *Capriccio*, *Orpheus* sounds with the same sonority as the *Concerto in D for Strings*, written the year before; haunting, Phrygian, largely for strings, but also with a very prominent and characteristic part for the harp. The middle section of the first *Air de danse* is very similar to the chordal writing of the first movement of the *Concerto*. The central point of the ballet is the *pas de deux*, as the Furies, moved by Orpheus' singing to the tormented souls in the under-world, bind his eyes and return Eurydice to him. Measured yet unequal melodies for the strings are followed by the woodwind, with the omnipresent *Symphony in C* motif intertwined.[1] A bar of silence marks the moment when Orpheus tears the blind-fold off, whereupon Eurydice falls dead. So Orpheus returns to earth—another interlude; this time a retrograde, more complex version of the first interlude, which separated the first and second scenes. So Orpheus is killed, but his song lives. The third scene is the apotheosis. Apollo appears, to carry his singing head heavenward. Two horns work out a two-part fugue—the material of the opening re-enacted—while a trumpet and two unison violins sing a long-drawn-out *cantus firmus*-like melody. The fugue is cut off by a harp phrase (after fig. 80); Orpheus is dead, but the accompaniment goes on compulsively. The fugue is then resumed, as if nothing had happened.

Much of *Orpheus* was mimed song; so to that extent opera followed naturally. With *The Rake's Progress* Stravinsky re-sumed the operatic problem where *Mavra* had left off. In the meantime Berg's *Wozzeck* had moved twentieth-century Euro-pean opera even further away from pre-Wagnerian clichés. Stravinsky did not set out to outflank Berg as a 'reformer'; instead he returned to those very clichés, of the Italian-Mozartian

[1] See p. 94.

classical style, that the contemporary German composers had sought to supersede.

Stravinsky's was a life-long acquaintance with opera; such works as *Ballo in maschera* and *Rigoletto* were familiar to him beyond the point where criticism of their obvious absurdities made any difference. While he was working on *The Rake's Progress* Mozart's *Così fan tutte* was his musical diet. He deliberately sought to re-vitalize the conventions of a period that many might have imagined were long since dead. The structure is built round arias, recitatives, choruses, ensembles, with a definite scheme of tonality. Generally speaking, prose is used for the recitatives, while the arias and ensembles are in verse. The orchestra is correspondingly small. As so often before, Stravinsky strove for a period-piece; in this case the conventions of *ostinato* accompaniment were more appropriate for the eighteenth century than polyphony, whose effect could be timeless, hieratic, as in the *Symphony of Psalms*.

The presence of Mozart is pervasive throughout *The Rake's Progress*. Not only is the orchestra one of classical proportions, including a harpsichord for the recitatives, but the daemonic atmosphere of the churchyard scene, as Rakewell and Shadow play cards, and the moralizing epilogue with which the opera ends, all point unmistakably to one model—*Don Giovanni*. *The Rake's Progress* marked the end, and the culmination, of a phase in Stravinsky's work—that 'incubation' generally known as neoclassicism. It was a universal musical phenomenon to which diverse composers subscribed, particularly those of the Franco-Russian tradition. Prokofiev's *Classical Symphony* is a well-known example; in England, Roberto Gerhard's *The Duenna* (1951) was another opera based on an eighteenth-century theme, also a comedy of manners.

Two stage works were written in Stravinsky's final phase, *Agon* and *The Flood*. *Agon* was started in 1953, the very moment of change to a serial style. Like *Le Rossignol* forty years before, it was laid aside, then resumed some years later, in 1956. During these years Webern's style was gradually embodied, in such pieces as the *Canticum Sacrum*. The subject of *Agon* is abstract, not classical or mythological, and the style is a fusion of gesture and music. Stravinsky used his newly discovered contrapuntal technique within an existing framework; the title suggests a dance-contest, with twelve dancers, eight female and four male, in different groupings. The orchestra is also graded and grouped, according to the timbre of the instruments—an aspect of serialism as he saw it that Stravinsky was to pursue in subsequent works. The twelve short dances (two groups of six, separated by an interlude) were modelled on a French seventeenth-century dance-manual, de Lauze's *Apologie de la danse*; indeed, an engraving of two trumpeters playing a *Bransle simple* suggested to Stravinsky the scoring for his own.

The assimilation of Webern's principles was a gradual process; in *Agon* Stravinsky has comprehended them and set them beside his own; the two have not yet fused, and metamorphosed into something else. The series is made up of three tetrachords; its use is quite free, and a strongly tonal underlay colours the score throughout. The same tetrachord, which contains features highly characteristic of Stravinsky's melodic style, begins the series of *The Flood*; indeed, these features also occur in the series for the other two large works written just before: *Movements* and *A Sermon, a Narrative and a Prayer*.[1]

The duration of *The Flood* (24 minutes) is comparable to *Agon* (20 minutes); but the score is much more complex and eventful, a compendium of theatrical effects. The totally chromatic 'representation of chaos' of the opening is resolved by the order of the series, spelt out by the harp, like a 'Jacob's Ladder', accompanied by its own diminution. Unlike *Agon*, *The Flood* is representational and symbolic. The brevity of the scenes is only partly

[1] See p. 138.

dictated by the concentrated requirements of television. Serialism makes for brevity, and moreover the narration both separates and links the episodes. Connecting episodes as such are dispensed with; and choreography is incidental.

As in *Agon*, the construction is formal, even symmetrical:

Bars		Scheme
1–7	Instrumental introduction	
8–61	Te Deum (1): Chorus	sung
62–167	The Creation: Narrator, God, Lucifer/Satan	
168–247	Melodrama: Narrator, God, Noah	spoken, sung
248–334	The building of the Ark: Instrumental	choreography
335–98	The Catalogue of the Animals: Noah, wife, narrator	spoken
399–456	The Flood: Instrumental	choreography
457–89	The Covenant of the Rainbow: God, Noah	
490–526	Introduction (reprise): Instrumental, Satan, Narrator	spoken, sung
527–79	Te Deum (2): Chorus	sung
580–2	Instrumental coda	

There are internal symmetries as well; the music for the flood is a mirror of itself, with the first half (bars 399–426) repeated in retrograde in the second half (428–55). (A similar mirror-process was used in the *Canticum Sacrum*.) The work begins and ends 'in church'; the prelude music first heard at the opening represents chaos, and when it recurs at the end (490) it represents sin—which is the subject of this musical play, not just the Noah-story. The flood stands for the atomic destruction of the world; the Ark is a symbol; so, structurally speaking, is the music.

12   Orchestral works

Like the stage works, Stravinsky's orchestral compositions run the entire gamut of his output, from the *Symphony in E flat* (1905–7) to the *Variations* (1963–4).

The extant early works, the *Symphony in E flat, Scherzo Fantastique* and *Feu d'artifice*, aptly serve to introduce the stage works, which started in 1910 and which thereafter occupied his chief attention until 1914. In spite of certain immature, academic features, such as an unexceptional and very ordinary sonata form in the first movement, and a somewhat pedantic rondo in the last, the symphony may be seen as a flexing of his technical muscles; it reveals a taste for orchestral exuberance, coupled with the use of melodic material derived from folk music. The *Scherzo,* which depicts the life-cycle of bees in a hive, is, most exceptionally for Stravinsky, somewhat four-square in its phrase construction—the flute melody at the opening of the slow section, starting at fig. 37, is a case in point; but ideas from this piece were to prove useful later; for instance, the string theme is used again in the *Firebird*, two bars before fig. 14 by the trumpets. The much shorter *Feu d'artifice*, also called a 'Fantasy', introduces more rhythmical flexibility than the symphony, as well as, once again, dramatic contrasts in the slow middle section. These qualities, as well as its length, suggested its use for a Futurist ballet (in Rome, 1917).

Not until 1920 did Stravinsky turn again to an orchestral work. Harmonically the *Symphonies of Wind Instruments* takes up where *Les Noces* left off; homogeneous groups of instruments discourse together in an austere ritual, polytonal and using additive rhythm—the very opposite of thematic development, in the traditional sense of the word. The music is built from opposing sound-blocks, in different tempi. The characteristic coda, the apotheosis, is made up of slow chords, in which tonic and dominant combine. Throughout the work, the metronome rate of each section is related systematically, either 72 or its sesquialtera 108. Evidently the sonority of contrasted wind instruments remained in Stravinsky's mind, for the flute melody, which first appears at fig. 6, was refashioned in the *Octet* for wind instruments, written some three years later, where it appears as a theme and variations.

As well as full symphonic works, Stravinsky wrote characteristically for the chamber orchestra. Two such works were transcriptions; the two *Suites* were transcribed from the eight easy piano-duet pieces, while the *Eight Instrumental Miniatures* were originally five-finger exercises for piano.

Suite No. 2 (1921) followed soon after the *Symphonies of Wind Instruments*, and indeed both suites show a marked leaning towards the wind sections of the orchestra. Apart from the *Andante* of *Suite No. 1*, all the important themes are given to them, and Stravinsky uses the strings mainly for accompaniment, or for the bass line. The *Valse* in *Suite No. 2* for wind septet, though written in homage to Erik Satie, might well have been written for the Ballerina in *Petrushka*; indeed, all eight movements, though simple, have the lightness of the fairground. This does not apply to the *Eight Instrumental Miniatures*, which are more elaborate and contrapuntal. In the process of transcription, the original easy piano pieces were rethought, and underwent 'rhythmic rewriting, phrase regrouping, new modulation'. An example of this may be seen in the *Larghetto* movement, which is in the style of a Berceuse. In the original piano version the opening seven-bar phrase is exactly repeated; in the instrumental version it is played first by a solo oboe, accompanied by flutes; it is then repeated with a second oboe in canon, by inversion at the twelfth, accompanied by two violins and two violas. Canon by inversion, and three-voice canon also occur in the first piece.

The other three works for chamber orchestra are among Stravinsky's best-loved scores. Both the *Dumbarton Oaks Concerto*, in E flat, and the later *Concerto in D* for strings make use of the central motif which was to come to full fruition in the *Symphony in C*:

Ex. 2

In the E flat concerto it occurs two bars before fig. 10 in the violin; in the *Concerto in D* violins and cellos sing it out at the beginning of the *Arioso* second movement.

The two concertos have similar features; both are Baroque-inspired, both last twelve minutes, both use a three-move-ment form. Moreover both develop rhythmic complexity; but 'Dumbarton Oaks' also uses *fugato* in the first and third movements, while in the other work Stravinsky was more pre-occupied with niceties of string-writing. The closing pages of 'Dumbarton Oaks', with the *basso ostinato*, are in direct line of descent from *Histoire du soldat*; the *Concerto in D*, on the other hand, has the dance-like sparkle of a divertimento. Metrical variety abounds, and unexpected modulation, such as the change from D to D flat at fig. 27.

The third chamber orchestra work, the *Danses Concertantes*, was composed a year after the *Symphony in C*, and was in some ways overshadowed by it. Numerous phrase-shapes and rhyth-mic motifs recall the symphony, which represented such a point-of-arrival for Stravinsky. For example, the following comparisons may be made:

Balanchine once remarked that everything Stravinsky wrote was suitable for the dance; certainly he was at one with the classical, abstract form, and would work out gestures and movements while listening to the music. In the case of *Danses Concertantes*, the varied phrase lengths and the plastic rhythms gave him the basis on which to develop his own choreographic movements. Nevertheless Stravinsky decidedly did not intend it for a ballet, and was not particularly favourable towards Balanchine's version. The choreographic titles of the movements were general, abstract, like the waltzes of Chopin, and not specific. The music itself 'reactivated the springs of *Jeu de cartes*'.

Stravinsky's works for full orchestra reached their highest point in the *Symphony in C* and the *Symphony in three movements*. The *Symphony in C*, his second symphony, bridges two worlds; the first two movements were written in Europe, 1938–1939, at a time of great personal grief; the third and fourth movements were written (1939–40) after his move to America. This change, and tension, are everywhere apparent in the symphony. The motif of the symphony, with which the first movement opens, sums up the twin aspects of Stravinsky's musical thinking hitherto (see p. 137), while the apotheosis with which the work concludes is a retrospective glance at a world which for him had receded. Of all Stravinsky's coda-sections, this one has a more intense poignancy than other comparable ones, such as *Apollo* or the *Symphony of Psalms*, because it has a personal as well as a musical and structural meaning.

Again, although all four movements use the same material, the first two movements contain no changes of metre; but extreme metrical irregularities appear in the third movement. The bustling bassoon solo at fig. 104 came to him 'with the neon glitter of the Californian boulevards from a speeding automobile':

Apart from the invention of new sonorities, such as the low writing for bassoons, horns and trombones in the introduction to the fourth movement, and of new structures in the last two movements, such as those arising from rhythmic and fugal developments, Stravinsky uses two main materials with which to exploit the motif; first the rhythm derived from it, next an ascending scale implied in it:

If the first two movements are comparatively orthodox in structure and tonality, the others complement them; the final apotheosis brings the two halves together, with G and C tonalities combined.

The *Symphony in three movements* employs a slightly larger orchestra than the *Symphony in C*: a third clarinet, double bassoon, bass drum, as well as piano and harp. Certain similar features link the two symphonies: the theme starting with a semitone, the use of scale passages, similar rhythmic patterns, the use of solo strings in the slow second movement, like a *concerto grosso*. Both were written over a number of years. Otherwise the later symphony is made of sterner stuff, and represents a further evolutionary stage. When Stravinsky played through parts of it to Alexandre Tansman in 1942 he saw it as a concerto for orchestra, with a *concertante* part for the piano. Structurally it is a succession of small *concertini* groups,[1] in chamber music style, like the *Symphonies of Wind Instruments*. The instruments divide at the development, starting at fig. 38 with the horn, and the climax consists of all the groups coming together at fig. 69, whereupon they separate again. The same principle of construction may be seen later in *Movements*.

At the recapitulation at fig. 88 Stravinsky reverses the order of themes. This procedure, unlike the *Symphony in C*, recalls the *Piano Sonata*. The first theme, when it is eventually reached at fig. 105, marks the point of arrival of the entire movement, Some of the scoring recalls *Le Sacre*, which Stravinsky was revising at this time. Harmonically, tonally and instrumentally the first and third movements are harsh, astringent; the slow movement is gentle, with brass reduced to quiet horns only, piano giving way to harp, chords of semitones giving way to

---

[1] Michael Tippett's *Concerto for Orchestra* (1963) is built also on this principle.

chords of whole tones. Cf. the 'canon by contrary motion' chords, figs. 124, 191:

If not a 'war symphony', it was written during the war. The mood is tragic, indignant; reflected in the semitonal harmony of the first and third movements. The harmonic repose of the middle movement is gradually dissolved by an interlude consisting of a succession of chords, gradually re-introducing the semitonal clashes, and thus preparing for the fury of the finale.

The third movement comes the nearest to having a 'war plot'; the march music predominates until the fugue, which is the stasis and the turning-point. The immobility at the beginning of the fugue (fig. 170—2) is comic; so to Stravinsky was the overturned arrogance of the Germans when their machine failed. The exposition of the fugue, and the end of the symphony, were associated in his mind with the allied victory. At fig. 172 the piano and harp are heard by themselves together for the first time. Other *concertino* episodes in this final movement are a canon for two bassoons, fig. 148, and a passage for string trio set against wind trio, fig. 154.

The conclusion of the work is tragic in its intensity; the final shattering chord, though grounded on D flat and not the expected C, is built from material already heard, right from the opening. The D flat itself springs from the Phrygian D flat of the second bar. The symphony is all of a piece.

Although the *Symphony in three movements* was begun in 1942, and occupied most of Stravinsky's attention in the war years, a number of slight orchestral pieces also date from that time. Some of them, such as the *Circus Polka, Four Norwegian Moods* and *Scherzo à la Russe*, need not be dwelt on for long; but the *Ode*, written in memory of Natalie Koussevitzky, is somewhat more substantial. The three movements are Eulogy, Eclogue, Epitaph; and of these the central one alone is *con moto*, flanked on either side by slow music. This reversal of the normal procedure was dictated by the *in memoriam* nature of the work. In spite of the solemn, chromatic music of the opening, the content of this eleven-minute work is concentrated into the final Epitaph, with much use of characteristic bitonality (see Ex. 7 overleaf).

Scènes de Ballet has a much closer association with the dance than *Danses Concertantes*. Stravinsky clearly visualized the dance-

Ex.7

construction of this plotless ballet, with instruments representing the dancers. In the *Pas de deux* the trumpet is associated with the male dancer, the horn with the female. The second *Pantomime* is an ensemble for the *corps de ballet*; the final *Pantomime* unites the solo dancers, after their separate dances just before; the whole company assembles for the finale. The apotheosis as usual contains the most characteristic music of the score, and also introduces a note of jubilation; it was written on 25th August 1944, the day of the liberation of Paris.

In its scoring, particularly the flute scoring of the first *Pantomime*, it recalls Tchaikovsky's *Pas de deux* (from *The Sleeping Beauty*), which Stravinsky had arranged in 1941 for small orchestra, for the Ballet Theatre, New York. As *Scènes de Ballet* is a period piece of Broadway, it opens with the 'Blues' chord in the introduction, at fig. 1. Another jazz-derived work was the *Ebony Concerto*, the word 'Ebony' referring to the African jazz culture of Harlem or Chicago that Stravinsky knew. It is a simple, pleasing work; a 'jazz *concerto grosso*', with a 'Blues' slow movement.

But thereafter, following the *Concerto in D* of 1946, it was many years before Stravinsky again wrote for the orchestra. In 1955 he wrote a very short piece on 'happy birthday to you', to mark the eightieth birthday, on 4th April that year, of his old friend the conductor Pierre Monteux. Apart from that, the demands of the new principles of serialism took Stravinsky's attention away from the symphony orchestra. In the event his final period gave rise to just one more orchestral work, the *Variations, Aldous Huxley in memoriam.*

The aphoristic conciseness of the music of this work, which continues in the style of *Movements,* is condensed into five minutes' duration. Innovation of timbre was nothing new to Stravinsky, ever since the *Firebird.* Now he applied it in the new context of a twelve-note series. As he says, 'the use of families and individuals in contrast is a principal projective element of the form [i.e. variations], especially of its symmetries and reversibles'.

The central feature of the work is an eleven-bar passage for twelve *ponticello* solo violins; the effect is like a musical mobile, in which the patterns seem to change perspective, with each part rhythmically distinct, playing *pp.* It is repeated, after a short woodwind episode, with the parts exchanged and inverted. After another longer episode of contrasting starkness, it is repeated again, and further varied, this time with twelve woodwind instruments. This threefold arch, which forms the main structure of the work, is preceded and followed by short phrases for various instrumental groups, with the piano used as a continuo. The leading solo roles are those of the flutes, bassoons and trombones.

The *Variations* are not variations of a theme, but diverse presentations of a series; the transpositions of the series are the equivalent of modulation in harmonic composition. The pulse remains constant (80), though the tempo is variable; rhythm and timbre are equally integral parts of the composer's scheme. No percussion instruments are used; that function is carried out by piano and harp together.

13   Works for solo instruments. Concertos

PIANO WORKS

One of Stravinsky's earliest works, if not the earliest, was for piano: the *Scherzo* (1902). He always composed at the piano; he himself was a polished player. It is not surprising, therefore, that piano works should figure prominently among the solo instrumental pieces. Almost all of them belong to the central, neo-classical period of his life, and the last of such major pieces was the *Sonata* for two pianos (1944). The piano as a solo instrument does not feature at all in the serial phase; only one work belongs to this period, *Movements*, for piano and orchestra, and this is specifically not a piano concerto.

After the early *Four Studies*, Op. 7, which is a profusion of neo-Romantic chromaticism, influenced chiefly by Scriabin, the central period works fall mainly into pairs; two collections of easy pieces, one for piano solo, *Les cinq doigts*, one for piano duet; two ragtime pieces; two solo works, and two duets, of sonata dimensions.

The sets of easy pieces, however short and unpretentious, are far from negligible; indeed both were later rescored for instruments (see Appendix B, VI). Of the eight piano-duet pieces, three were written before *Renard* (Polka, March, Valse), and were caricatures of Diaghilev, Casella and Satie respectively; the remaining five were short colour-pieces for Stravinsky's children, Theodore and Mika. In first choosing to write duets, Stravinsky had in mind that Diaghilev was also a pianist, if not a very advanced one. We may imagine him, in the three pieces, playing the easy left-hand part, while the composer played the (rather more interesting) right.

Ragtime is a transcription from the version for 11 instruments, while *Piano-Rag-Music* is an original piano piece. Both belong in the *Histoire du soldat* camp, as short, brilliant period pieces, or 'concert portraits'. The same applies to the slightly earlier *Étude* for pianola, which recalls impressions of Spain, and to the much later *Tango* (1940). Stravinsky was adept at capturing, satirizing and caricaturing in this way the mood or the period of his surroundings.

Both the *Sonata* and the *Serenade* start from classical points of reference. In the *Sonata* Stravinsky takes the texture and mannerism of early Beethoven and Chopin in the Adagietto, and of a Bach two-part invention in the finale, as he steers the music into a harmonic and metrical style of his own choosing. The brilliance of the pianism, most of it in two parts, results largely from the gradation of different touches, from *secco* to *legatissimo*, at all dynamic levels. The *Serenade* is more chordal, and opens with a reference to Chopin's second Ballade (Op. 38). The movements (Hymne, Romanza, Rondoletto, Cadenza Finale) are the equivalent of a suite or partita of the eighteenth century; the piece is 'polarized about A'.

The *Concerto for two pianos*, in duration and content, is the most substantial of all Stravinsky's piano works. The first movement, written in 1931, immediately after the *Violin Concerto*, was separated by three years from the rest, which followed after *Persephone*. The work, which was Stravinsky's favourite, uses the two pianos equally, and is very much of a show-piece for concert use. Its proportions are symphonic. The second movement (Notturno) and third movement (Four Variations) were originally in reverse order. The Four Variations are the *scherzando* section of the work, followed by the contrasting slow Prelude of the last movement. The fugue subject of the finale (Pre-

lude and Fugue) is the theme of the preceding Four Variations
—a procedure he was to use again later, for instance in the
Septet.

Stravinsky was 'steeped in the variations of Beethoven and
Brahms' at this time. The Notturno movement, which he describes as 'after-dinner music: a digestive to the larger movements', is an extended, decorated aria, which uses an *ostinato*
figure, later a dotted rhythm, which at the end reveals itself as a
counter-subject to the main theme, which recurs only in the
final bars. The effect is of great spaciousness.

The *Sonata for two pianos*, on the other hand, is a slighter
work, in content and texture. Since it comes between the two
great symphonies, it is not surprising that echoes of the *Symphony in C* motif should be heard in it—starting with the opening theme in the very first bar. Its three-movement form recalls
the earlier *Sonata* for solo piano, except that in this case the first
and third movements are gentle, not brilliant, and the finale is
surprisingly short. Stravinskyan ingenuities abound; for instance
in the first movement, after the first subject, key and metre
suddenly switch before the second, which is a countersubject to
an *ostinato* based on the first subject, with a *leggiero* bass in
augmentation. Again as in the *Symphony in C*, Stravinsky uses
a harmony based on tonic and dominant sounding simultaneously, with the leading-note very prominent.

Stravinsky wrote three works for piano and orchestra, all very
different. The *Concerto* for piano and wind instruments begins
with all the solemnity of a funeral march, but the entry of the solo
piano heralds an abrupt change to a percussive *Allegro*. The
piano style is brittle, whether chords, octaves or single notes,
and its regularity is mechanical; the *style perlé* is reserved for
brief cadenza-moments in the slow movement. The third movement is the most complex—a reversal of classical procedure—
and the piano acts as something of a continuo in holding
together the contrapuntal elaboration. The themes are tailor-

made to the various instruments (such as the tuba solo at fig. 77—4), and earlier material is recalled at the end.

The *Capriccio* is less *martellato* in style than the earlier *Concerto*. Stravinsky still revels in cascades of notes, but they are more graceful in their variety and flexibility. The overall pace is very quick, the overall mood one of brilliance, offset by the occasional use of chamber-music scoring for solo instruments, and setting the piano with different groups. If the *Andante rapsodico* takes Bach as its starting point, the final *Capriccio* contains, as a contrast, a fox-trot trumpet tune (at fig. 88). The quotation of other composers' works was part of the game of neo-classicism, and was very common practice, particularly at this time, among Stravinsky's French contemporaries, and others. Poulenc's *Concerto for two pianos* (1932) is an example, drawing as it does for its sources on Mozart, Chopin, Saint-Saëns, Balinese folk-music—and Stravinsky himself.

The third concerted work, *Movements* for piano and orchestra, was written much later, and stands apart in every aspect from the other two, because its aesthetic basis differs. It represents the first application of serialism in a purely orchestral score, and as such marks a turning-point in Stravinsky's output. Though its duration (ten minutes) is half that of the *Capriccio*, and the orchestra is much reduced, the degree of 'eventuation' is much greater, more concentrated. It is the most complex of his serial works. And just as the serialism of *Agon* had led to the variability of other factors than the notes of the series (the dances themselves, for instance, and the twelve dancers), so in *Movements* every aspect of the composition, not merely pitch, was guided by serial form; even the use of a defined timbre for short orchestral interludes. But total variation of the material, in all its aspects, results, curiously, in total sameness of overall mood. The work lacks, for instance, that earlier *scherʒando* brilliance, which is inconsistent with serialism.

The series, which can partly be traced to the *Symphony in C* motif, consists essentially of four groups of three adjacent notes. For this reason the interval of the minor second is prevalent throughout the work, as well as its corollaries the minor ninth, with which the first movement opens, and the minor sixteenth, with which it closes.

In the widest sense, of construction and rhythm, the five movements may be said to bear the same sort of relationship to each other as the movements of a classical symphony or sonata. In the first, the opening section is repeated, like an exposition; after a slow passage the series appears again in its original form (bar 42), like a recapitulation. This repetition is comparable with the repeat of sections in *Threni*, such as the passage starting at bars 42, 88 and 142; also with *A Sermon, a Narrative and a Prayer*, in which bars 27–34 recur at bars 64–71, to make a conclusion. These works were written just before, and just after, *Movements*; in each case repetition serves a structural purpose, to replace the structures of discarded tonality.

The second movement is played predominantly by piano and strings, the third by piano and wind, with the brass alone in the last four bars. The fourth contains the only orchestral *tutti*, with all eight hexachords used simultaneously, while in the fifth Stravinsky reverts again to the segmentation of the orchestra, using all the instruments separately, except the oboe and bassoon. The work is not a concerto so much as a study in the grouping together of various instruments with the piano, which plays very nearly throughout. Stravinsky's original title was 'Concerto for pianoforte and groups of instruments'. The piano appears in different contexts, as the voices had in *Threni*.

The intervals of the series are attracted by tonality. As Stravinsky says, he composed vertically, 'and that is, in one sense at least, to compose tonally'. Structure, which gives the music a sense of identity, can be created without tonality; by a return to a starting-point, for instance. But tonality cannot be ignored, even if the sound of *Movements* transcends any existing or accepted point of reference. It represents the further point reached by Stravinsky in that respect; also the most abstruse rhythmically. The piece consists of a constant variation, and paraphrase, of the direct statement of the material.

In April 1963 Balanchine made it into a ballet, to which Stravinsky's reaction was that 'to see it is to hear the music with one's eyes . . . the performance was like a tour of a building for which I had drawn the plans but never explored the result'.

In the piano works as a whole, which are unique in that, with the exception of *Movements*, he himself played and recorded them,[1] Stravinsky invented a new kind of *espressivo* pianism. The chief characteristics of it were extremes of touch, graded and contrasted, coupled with the cleanest articulation, at all dynamic levels, even in *sostenuto*. Matching the nature of the material, his style of playing stood at the opposite pole to Romanticism.

Very few directions for performance appear in the music, and in particular very sparing use is made of the pedals; indeed the *Sonata* and *Serenade* are played without pedals. Such a granular clarity is part of the conception of the music, even in *legato* sections, such as the *Adagietto* of the *Sonata*. Moreover the tempi in *vivace*, such as the finale of the *Sonata*, or the variations of the Concerto for two pianos, are never so fast that the articulation of the smallest notes is sacrificed. The first movement of that work derives its *vivace* quality partly from the rapid articulation of repeated notes—a favourite device—partly from short, *détaché* chords; the opening of the *Notturno* also puts this technique to good effect.

The use of a pointed left-hand *staccato* is further illustrated in the *Rondoletto* of the *Serenade*. Single chords, *sf, secco*, made

---

[1] He also recorded the *Duo Concertant* and other violin pieces with Dushkin.

possible partly by the fact that Stravinsky's wide stretch easily covered a tenth, are occasionally used to mark the cadences in this movement; they also feature prominently in the *Romanza*. The *legato* of the finale comes as all the more of a contrast.

That his piano works encompassed both spaciousness and brilliance is amply illustrated in the largest of them, the *Concerto for two pianos*. The *Notturno* is a foretaste of the *Andante* of the *Symphony in three movements*; moreover the same material occurs in different movements. This common device occurs again in the *Capriccio*, not just in the use of themes, but also of motifs; for instance the falling semitone of the opening *Presto*:

appears throughout the final *Allegro capriccioso* as a rising one:

The piano writing in this work also contains a recurrence of certain features of the *Serenade*; for instance the passage in thirds at fig. 78.

Stravinsky was a most sensitive pianist; but he could not allow a career of piano-playing to take him away from composition. As his son Soulima gradually began to be known as a performer, he himself played less and less.

OTHER WORKS

Next to the piano, the violin chiefly claimed Stravinsky's attention; he wrote two important large-scale works for it, both for Samuel Dushkin, with whom he performed and recorded as a duo.

The *Violin Concerto* came after the *Capriccio*, and something of the same *vivace* quality spills over from the one to the other. The model, as before, was Bach, particularly the Bach of the Concerto for two violins, more than the established classical concertos; the two-part writing for solo violin and bassoon at fig. 94 is a case in point:

The titles of movements (Toccata, Aria I and II, Capriccio) are also Bachian.

The brilliance of the concerto stems largely from the virtuoso writing for the soloist; the material itself is simple. Two ideas make up the first movement; one, at the opening, consisting of the diatonic scale of D, in thirds, the other at fig. 7 more chromatic, in fourths. A development figure, based on the main subject, is transformed into something subtle by a displaced accent at fig. 29; thereafter it is made into something fresh, and more melodic, by augmentation in the solo part at fig. 33.

Another very characteristically Stravinskyan touch occurs at the end of the concerto, with the *Histoire du soldat* passage starting at fig. 123, which gradually changes from $\frac{2}{8}$ to $\frac{3}{8}$; this process, though it begins at fig. 129, only reaches completion at the end of the work.

If the solo writing in the *Violin Concerto* is rhythmically taut and percussive, in the *Duo Concertant* the violin is allotted a more linear part—this in spite of occasional metrical innovations, particularly in episodes of the *Gigue*, and occasional echoes of the *Histoire du soldat* style, such as parts of *Eglogue I*. The two instruments move horizontally, with complementary harmonies, and the piano never blankets those of the violin. Harmonic movement in the violin, such as in *Eglogue I*, is set against a simple *ostinato* in the piano part, or else single notes. The pulse-unit in the *Dithyramb* led to notation difficulties, as it did in the *Notturno* movement of the *Concerto for two pianos*, written shortly afterwards. As the *Duo* came between *Apollo* and *Persephone*, when Stravinsky was preoccupied with Greek themes, the movements have classical titles.

The *Elegy* for solo viola, also written for the violin a fifth higher, serves as a pendant to the two larger works. It was written at the request of Germain Prévost in memory of Alphonse Onnou, the founder of the Pro Arte Quartet. Played *con sordino* throughout, in spite of the fugal middle section, which builds to a considerable climax before the reprise of the opening, the intensely varied music is like a preview of the *pas de deux* in *Orpheus*. It was aptly choreographed by Balanchine for two dancers.

Ensemble and chamber music.
Songs for solo voice

ENSEMBLE AND CHAMBER MUSIC

Stravinsky's works for various small ensembles are for the most part short, aphoristic. They are summaries, and in the nature of technical studies. The *Three Pieces for String Quartet*, for instance, are a source from which he later drew; coming as they did at a moment in the composer's life when the war had put an end to one phase of his work, and presented him with uncertainties about what was to follow, they marked, as he says, 'an important change' in his art. The work is not a string quartet in the normally understood, classical sense of the word; rather is it a setting-down in the form of studies of some ideas that are basic to his musical language, using the medium of a string quartet. The features of his melodic style, which were shortly to find their outlet in the Russian works of the war years, and which later reached such maturity in the *Symphony in C* motif, are already apparent in the first piece, with its constant repetition of a very simple four-note melody.

When these pieces were orchestrated, the first three in 1917, the last in 1929, as *Four Studies for Orchestra*, they were given titles: *Danse, Excentrique, Cantique*. (The fourth piece, *Madrid*, was scored from the *Study for pianola*.) The third piece, with its liturgical invocation, particularly pleased Stravinsky. It is much clearer in the orchestrated version, in which it was slightly altered by the augmentation of the triplet notation of the first and last bars. The use of the piano in the other pieces brings echoes of *Petrushka*.

The *Concertino* for string quartet differs in that it is cast in one single movement, lasting six minutes, and is more specifically a concert work for particular performers. Its structure is a free sonata *Allegro*, with a cadenza for the first violin, starting at fig. 11. This work also was rescored later, as the *Concertino for twelve instruments*, when the *obbligato* was redistributed between a violin and a violoncello; and there is also considerable rebarring, to bring out the harmony and phrasing more clearly.

During the final period of his life Stravinsky wrote just two short but characteristic pieces in this category, both in 1959, following *Movements*. The *Epitaphium*, 'for the tombstone of Prince Max Egon zu Fürstenburg', followed the death in April that year of the founder and patron of the *Donaueschingen Musiktage*, with which Stravinsky had been associated from its earliest days. The music is a sequence of short antiphons or funeral responses, between a harp in its bass register and a wind duet (flute and clarinet) in the treble. There are four short antiphonal strophes for the harp, four for the wind duet, and each strophe is a complete statement of the series, in one of its four versions.

The second little piece of that year was the *Double Canon*, *Raoul Dufy in memoriam*. Unlike the other, this was not a personal tribute, as the composer and the painter never met. It was written in Venice in September 1959, in response to a private request for an autograph. The double canon is made by the two violins, who play the series at an interval of a major second, later its retrograde inversion, and the viola and violoncello, who play the retrograde version of the series at an interval of a minor seventh. It forms a ternary structure, beginning and ending with two violin parts, with a central section made up of fuller four-part texture. The work recalls the earlier string-quartet canons in the *In memoriam Dylan Thomas*; indeed the five-note row on which that work is based is melodically similar to the series of the *Double Canon*.[1]

[1] See p. 138.

In contrast to these miniatures, two ensemble pieces are much more substantial—the *Octet* for wind instruments, and the *Septet*. Though separated by thirty years, they have certain points in common; both are strictly formal compositions, based on pure counterpoint; both contain variations; both represent the start of a fresh phase of Stravinsky's work, the first neo-classical, the second serial. At the time of composing the *Octet* Stravinsky also wrote an article in a magazine, which amounts to a manifesto of some of the tenets of his neo-classical aesthetic.[1] He found that the wind, by their very nature, lend themselves to a certain rigidity of form, which exactly suited his 'objective' view of music. Contrasts of movement and volume alone determine the music; not nuance or 'interpretation'.

The 'theme-and-variations' structure was one much favoured by him, from *Pulcinella* to the *Variations for orchestra*. But the *Pulcinella* variations are not an original set of variations on a theme; the first of these occurs in the *Octet*. The theme is characteristic of Stravinsky, with reiteration of a small number of notes in a pattern, using the second 'mode of limited transposition.'[2] The variations follow the melody quite exactly, and the last one is a *fugato*, in which the subject inverts the intervals of the theme, and the instruments enter in pairs.

The variations in the *Septet* take the form of a passacaglia, in which the theme is repeated in the bass, altered with octave transpositions. The counterpoints are in the form of canons. The eight notes making up the passacaglia theme, which is made up of two tetrachords, each consisting of the first four notes of the

---

[1] 'Some ideas about my *Octuor*', *The Arts*, January 1924. Reprinted in White, op. cit., p. 528.
[2] In its tenth transposition. See my *Contemporary Music*, p. 74.

third 'mode of limited transposition', are used as an eight-note series for the final *Gigue*—the first admission by Stravinsky of this fresh principle of construction; but in this case it is heavily overlaid with the most intricate fugal counterpoint.

SONGS FOR SOLO VOICE

Stravinsky's songs form a small but important part of his output. By far the greater number were written before 1919; many during the war, when his years in Switzerland were largely devoted to his rediscovering the Russian language. There followed a long gap in song-writing, of over thirty years, until the Shakespeare settings of 1953; after which only four more original songs were written—one 'sacred ballad', two *in memoriam*, the fourth as a final tribute to his wife.

Stravinsky's first songs were settings of Pushkin, in the form of a vocal suite, dedicated to Rimsky-Korsakov—*The Faun and the Shepherdess*, for voice and orchestra. They show a Debussyish lyricism, though rhythmically and harmonically straightforward. Looking back on them later, Stravinsky described them as 'like Wagner in places, like Tchaikovsky's *Romeo and Juliet* in other places—but never like Rimsky-Korsakov, which must have troubled that master, and like Stravinsky not at all'.

More a foretaste of characteristic Stravinsky were the three little *Souvenirs de mon enfance*, also started as early as 1906. They were *plaisanteries* for his own enjoyment, in which for the first time he made use of Russian popular texts; as such the songs were the precursor of several important later works. *Pribaoutki* and *Berceuses du chat* were further such examples, which differ in that they were originally written for voice and instruments, not voice and piano, and make use of some onomatopœia, such as the oboe and clarinet cadenza at the end of the first song of *Pribaoutki*, to represent the drinking habits of Uncle Armand. None of the

Russian songs contain folk material; the melodic line is built round the repetition of a small number or pattern of notes, in irregular phrase-formations.

The Verlaine songs (1910), written for Stravinsky's brother Goury, show, perhaps inevitably, a strong Debussy influence, and French Impressionist atmosphere generally. The two Balmont songs, on the other hand, written the following year, are much more original, however diminutive their scale. In 1954 Stravinsky orchestrated them, using the same instruments as he had used for the *Three Japanese Lyrics* (1913), which are one of the highlights of his early songs. Not only is each song compressed and terse in its three-fold structure, but the group as a whole also form a ternary shape and have great formal precision; the first and third songs are balanced by mood, tempo, text and dynamics, while a climax of brilliance is reached in the middle song, *Mazatsumi*.

That Stravinsky should turn to a setting of Japanese was not surprising; Orientalism was common at this time and shared, among many others, by Debussy and Ravel. But the Schoenbergian chromaticism of the *Japanese Lyrics* was something new to Stravinsky's *melos*. He uses almost a twelve-note texture. This was the result of his hearing Schoenberg's *Pierrot Lunaire* the year before (1912) in Berlin, and later again in Paris. But however much he approved the scoring of this work, he found Schoenberg's atonal aesthetic unacceptable, and had no further use for it for over forty years—until after Schoenberg's death in 1951, by which time Webern, who died in 1945, had pointed the way beyond the twelve-note style, towards serialism.

Although certain effects of instrumentation in the Shakespeare songs (1953) recall the earlier style, the melodic line could not be more different. Gone are the terseness and urgency of the *Quatre Chants Russes* or *Pribaoutki*; in their place a melodic line of wider-ranging intervals, and one that is on an equality, contrapuntally speaking, with the three-part accompaniment.

In *Berceuses du chat* the three clarinets form a balanced chorus, high, medium and low; the homogeneous vocal line practically amounts to a fourth clarinet. So in the Shakespeare songs the voice is treated like another treble instrument, to which the contrasting tone of the viola is heard largely in canon. But something of the earlier melodic style is recaptured by the first of the *in memoriam* songs, *In memoriam Dylan Thomas*, in so far as a five-note row is repeated, in various forms, which gives the music a compactness lacking in the Shakespeare songs (see p. 113). Moreover, since the five-note row is built round two minor thirds, this lends also an intensity to the very short *Elegy for J.F.K.*; it is ternary in structure, and the opening stanza, covered by the twelve-note series, is repeated at the end. The simple two-part writing of *The Owl and the Pussy-cat* rests on a strict canon between voice and piano, the latter in augmentation. The composer's ideas for its performance are equally definite: the song 'should be impersonated, a little hooted, a little mee-owed, a little grunted for the pig'.

One work stands apart, the sacred ballad *Abraham and Isaac*, not only for its religious nature, nor the fact that it was dedicated to the people of Israel in appreciation of his visit there in 1962, but for its dramatic scope, and the concentrated expressiveness of the solo melodic line. The setting of a Genesis text places the ballad in succession to the other biblical works. It followed directly after *The Flood*. The discovery of the sound of Hebrew excited Stravinsky, and the verbal and musical accentuations coincide—which is rare for him.

The six sections follow without interruption, with successively slower pulsation. Smaller units, or cells, are stressed rather than the full series, which in any case is scalic, thus allowing for an occasional melisma in the vocal line. The first of these occurs on the name 'Isaac' (35); it is subsequently echoed by the orchestra when the name recurs (113, 150), and also in the flute cadenza (89) with which the orchestral interlude begins.

The repetition of adjacent notes recalls the melodic style of earlier works, such as *Les Noces*.

The structure is marked by symmetries, canon, and 'serial verticals', or homophonic passages for groups of instruments, at certain dramatic moments of the story; for instance the strings (*tremolo, ponticello*) for God's voice (69); and low wind for the preparation of the sacrifice (106). As a single voice is used, even for the dialogue, such devices among others not only help to differentiate the characters, but point the tonal bias of the work, which is round the note C sharp.

15   Cantatas and choral works

Next to the stage works, Stravinsky's choral compositions occupy a central position in his output. Starting with the *Cantata* (1952), his serial phase was largely given over to religious choral works, which for their substance and importance provide a balance with the dramatic works of the first phase of his career. Although the *Cantata* is not a serial work, it marks a change from previous methods, and relies for its construction on those principles of inversion, canon and so on, which are the mainstay of serial, as distinct from tonal, composition. This work therefore forms the dividing line between the seven choral works of the final period and the eight that had gone before.

The choral works of the earlier period, of which seven are sacred, one secular, extend from *Zvezdoliki* to the *Mass. Zvezdoliki* (1911) is a setting for male-voice chorus and large orchestra of a text by Balmont, two of whose poems Stravinsky had just used for solo songs. At a concert in 1913 devoted to contemporary music, it was given as representative of Russia. Other composers were, from Germany, Schoenberg; from France, Debussy; from Hungary, Bartók. In this piece, suggestive of Scriabin, the Symbolist imagery of the Last Judgment led Stravinsky to a combination of Debussy-like richness of sound, coupled with a style of dramatic recitation, that was to reappear much later in his choral works. In dedicating this work to Debussy (and, later, the *Symphonies of Wind Instruments* to his memory) Stravinsky was overtly acknowledging the leading position that Debussy held in Western music at that time, which was so keenly felt by himself, particularly in the Verlaine songs and other early works. Indeed, the direction in which Stravinsky turned in the 1920s, towards neo-classical instrumental music, was partly the result of Debussy's reverting to 'absolute music' in his last years.

The secular choral work of this time, *Four Russian Peasant Songs* ('Soucoupes—Saucers') for unaccompanied female voices, affords short, diverting examples of Stravinsky's popular style. They belong in the colourful world of the *Trois histoires*, or *Les Noces*, with short, incisive melodic patterns, repeated with varied phrase-shapes. Like the Balmont solo songs, they were also rescored much later, and set against a chorus of four horns.

The culmination of Stravinsky's choral works of the inter-war period was reached with the *Symphony of Psalms*. It was surrounded, as if by its satellites, by shorter religious pieces; three simple, unaccompanied settings, in Slavonic, intended for liturgical use in the Russian Orthodox Church: *Pater noster*, *Credo* and *Ave Maria*. These were later published with a Latin text. The first of them marks not only Stravinsky's reverting to the Orthodox Church, but the rediscovery of the religious depths of his nature, which inspired his choral music from now on.

The *Symphony of Psalms* stands out from its surroundings, majestic and exultant, like a mountain peak. The 'laudate' motto uses for the first time as such the motif central to Stravinsky's melodic idiom, which was later to form the core of the *Symphony in C*.[1] No composer could write such a work without a very secure, rock-like, religious faith. Stravinsky sought to give voice to compulsion, exaltation, not lyrical-sentimental feeling. Starting, as he had with the short church pieces, with the text in Slavonic, he soon switched to the Latin of the Vulgate. The three parts of the symphony are continuous.

The third section was written first, with its rhythmic *ostinato* derived from 'laudate Dominum', and the sequences of two

---

[1] See p. 137.

minor thirds, joined by a major third, which are the root idea of the whole work, and which first appear in the trumpet and harp motif at fig. 3 + 5. They are used as *ostinati* in the first section, the prelude; they lead to the two fugue subjects of the second section: first the instrumental fugue, starting with four treble instruments (flutes, oboes), next the choral fugue, accompanied by an orchestral statement of the first fugue. After an *a cappella* section, at fig. 10 + 1, both fugues combine as the choir declaim (*ff*) 'Et immisit in os meum canticum novum'.

The *Alleluia* at the start of the next section is that 'new song'; the rest of the introductory slow music is a prayer to the Russian image of the infant Christ, with orb and sceptre. This music is also used later to provide the conclusion of the symphony, the characteristic apotheosis, starting at fig. 22; in this case the 'calm of praise', built over a four-note ground bass with piano, harp and timpani. The *Allegro* part of this third section begins and ends with an orchestral *sinfonia*; it was inspired 'by a vision of Elijah's chariot climbing the Heavens', of which the triplet rhythm for horns and piano at fig. 18 is a literal representation. But what chiefly concerned Stravinsky were the sounds of the syllables. As usual he regulated prosody in his own way.

Two other 'middle-period' works were written in America: *Babel,* and the *Mass*. Though short, *Babel* is a perfectly structured unity, finishing with a coda-apotheosis as the last of its four sections.[1] The narrator speaks a selected part of Genesis, and the male-voice chorus are given the words of God. As a whole, the work serves as a preface to the more important *Mass* which was shortly to follow.

Stravinsky's intention was to write a 'real' Mass; that is to say, one that could be used in the regular liturgy of the Roman Catholic Church. As he wished to accompany it with wind instruments, its use would be proscribed in the Russian Orthodox

[1] Starting at fig. 27.

Church. In the *Symphony of Psalms* he used boys' voices; so here also he called for children's voices, because of their 'coolness of timbre'. He avoided using the organ, as it was an instrument he disliked, because of its 'legato sostenuto and its blur of octaves, as well as the fact that the monster never breathes'. Wind instruments, on the other hand, 'breathe very attractively'; and so he chose a balanced choir of five woodwind and five brass. The instruments are used independently, not doubling the voice; also occasionally for intonation, such as the lead in to fig. 50.

The *Credo,* the statement of Christian belief, is the centre of the *Mass*, with the shorter movements acting as a frame for it. It is full, homophonic, in *parlando* style, only changing to a legato polyphony for the final 'Amen'. Stravinsky reached back for his musical sources for this Mass beyond Bach, to the Middle Ages, and the age of plainchant. About the low state of twentieth-century liturgical music he had few illusions ('the tradition has been lost'), but the time when he wrote his *Mass* (1947) was also an 'Alexandrian' period, one of increasing awareness of the earlier periods of music. This was largely reflected in research by musicologists such as Gustave Reese, Willi Apel and Manfred Bukofzer.[1] Though he disclaims any specific influence in his *Mass*, Stravinsky was very sensitive to this trend, and he became increasingly interested in early composers, such as Monteverdi and Gesualdo, in subsequent years.

The *Kyrie* and *Gloria* were written in 1944, three years before the rest. The 'solo' and 'full' antiphony, of the *Gloria* and *Sanctus,* are an application of the responsorial singing of Gregorian psalms, which was Jewish in origin. In the *Gloria* the two solo voices lead into a vocal *organum* (at fig. 17), while at the corresponding point in the *Sanctus* (fig. 45 + 2) there is a sudden and dramatic change to the Phrygian mode ('pleni sunt coeli'),

---

[1] Reese's *Music in the Middle Ages* first appeared in 1940; Apel's *Harvard Dictionary* in 1944; Bukofzer's *Music in the Baroque Era* in 1947.

and a four-part fugal section leading to a *tutti* climax ('Hosanna') at fig. 48.[1] Not till the final *Agnus Dei* does Stravinsky write for voices and instruments antiphonally, with contrasting blocks of music, gradually lessening in volume.

Although the *Cantata*, which marks the transition to the final period, is secular, the seven choral works which follow it are all sacred. Some of the vocal material of the *Cantata* is similar to that of the Mass; the Phrygian choral writing of *A Lyke-Wake Dirge* for instance. Moreover the archaism of the *Mass*, that quest for pre-classical, mediaeval sources, is here pursued further, in Stravinsky's choice of anonymous fifteenth- and sixteenth-century English lyrics. The body of the work is two *Ricercars*, by which term Stravinsky understands simply a composition in canonic style. The elaboration developed in this piece, particularly in the second *Ricercar* ('tomorrow shall be my dancing day') was further pursued by him in the *Septet* the following year.

Both the *Cantata*, and the next choral work, the *Canticum Sacrum*, are transitional works, as Stravinsky gradually discovered and assimilated the radical implications for himself of Webern's technique. The *Canticum* is a composite work, incorporating features from many others, including the ritualistic severity of the *Mass*. But the counterpoint is harmonic, and intervals of the series are attracted by tonality; this is due to Stravinsky's hearing increased sonorous and harmonic possibilities in the rules and restrictions of serialism. The five sections of the work correspond to the five domes of St Mark's Cathedral in Venice, for which it was specifically written and designed, from every point of view. Even the staccato brass chords in the first and fifth sections may be heard as thrusting the tone forward into the resonant acoustic of a great cathedral; the ensemble includes, for the first and last time in his whole output, an organ. The all-important cyclic formal design is as follows:

[1] *Cf.* the final section of *Orpheus*, horn music between figs. 144 and 145.

Section		Theme	Scoring, material used
		Dedicatio	Tenor and Baritone soli. Plainsong derivation.
Tonal	I	'Euntes in mundum' (Jesus's command)	*Chorus*, full, homophonic *Orchestra* antiphonal with organ. Tonal progression B♭–D
	II	Surge Aquilo (Love-lyric)	Tenor & solo instruments, Flute, Cor Anglais, Harp (Double Bass interjections sound D tonality)
Freely Serial	III	Ad tres virtutes Hortationes (Charity—Hope —Faith)	Ternary structure, A—B—C; each introduced by organ refrain and short sinfonia A choral canons B dialogue between soloists (T.B.) and chorus (S.A.) C choral canons (inversion of organ refrain)
	IV	Brevis motus cantilenae (St Mark's belief illustrated)	Baritone solo and chorus. B. solo opens with note of organ refrain in III. *Orchestra* very light, largely the notes of D tonality. bars 284–306 pedal D, leading into V
Tonal	V	Illi autem profecti (Jesus's command carried out)	*Chorus* full, homophonic *Orchestra* antiphonal with organ. Movement is a retrograde of I, beginning with the chord at the end of I. Tonal progression D–B♭

Having thus prepared the ground with the *Canticum,* Stravinsky was ready for his first completely serial choral work the following year. The series of *Threni* contains numerous thirds, major and minor, and this results in triadic vertical combinations. In the construction of a serial polyphony the composer chiefly exploits canon, which opens for him an infinity of new harmonic possibilities. The adoption of such a contrapuntal-serial style in no way solves structural problems; on the contrary, it creates different ones. New structures are called for to satisfy the new constructional logic, which in Stravinsky's case was also subordinate to the logic of his ear.

The work is in three sections—*De Elegia Prima, De Elegia Tertia, De Elegia Quinta*—of which the middle one, like the *Canticum,* is the longest, and is itself divided into three: *Querimonia* (complaint), *Sensus spei* (the feeling of hope), *Solacium* (comfort). The 'Lamentations of Jeremiah' occur in both the Jewish and the Roman Churches, and are sung in Holy Week. Stravinsky knew the work of Palestrina, Byrd, Tallis and other Renaissance composers, and made his setting primarily vocal; the orchestra is of secondary importance. It is never used in *tutti,* and instead is deployed in different groups with different voices.

As in the *Canticum,* there is an introduction by a vocal duet; but in this case the upper voice gives out the series in its original form, the lower voice in its inverted form. Stravinsky admits a certain licence in his use of the series; he repeats sections, he repeats notes (particularly in the second section, *sensus spei,* starting at bar 194), he alters the order, he omits notes; in the vertical combination of parts, which are not in rhythmic unison, he omits bar-lines (such as Diphona I and II, bars 66, 112), a procedure which continues the freedom of the canonic choruses in the third section of the *Canticum Sacrum.* But the use of canon is more pronounced in *Threni,* starting with the tenor and bugle at bar 42; in the *Querimonia* it is used progressively to build a choral polyphony—in 2 at bar 174, in 3 at bar 180, in 4, a double canon, at bar 189.

The Coda, or apotheosis of the work, at the words 'converte nos' (bar 405), presents the series in seven different versions, shared between voices and horns; it also brings the music to its extreme moment of tonal polarization—its spiritual as well as its musical conclusion.

The text of *Threni* had been taken from the Old Testament; that of *A Sermon, A Narrative and A Prayer* was taken from the New. After the extreme complexities of *Movements*, which intervened between the two choral works, Stravinsky reverted in this one to a rhythmically simple style. Once again the orchestra is divided into groups, according to timbre and pitch, and is used sparingly. The complexities and fragmentation to which serialism naturally leads, are best suited to instruments in solo, not to large *tutti* sections; to polyphony not homophony.

As in *Threni*, repetition is used as a structural means. The first movement is in two equal halves, each starting with an instrumental introduction. The refrain, in a measured *parlando* by the chorus, occurs twice (at bars 27, 64).

The second movement, the largest, is narrated by a speaker, and sung only by the contralto and tenor soloists, whose parts are joined into one, without the chorus. Most of the melodic entries are the retrograde form of the series (for instance the contralto melody at bar 82); but at the climax moment at bar 172 the tenor sings the original form, followed immediately by the retrograde. The moment of dramatic excitement which ensues is marked by the splitting up of the series, as well as the voices, into small particles, which can form chords.

The third movement closes the work over the suggestion of a quasi-ground bass, recalling the final *Alleluia* of the *Symphony of Psalms*. Double basses, harp, piano and three tam-tams (high, middle and low), in rhythmic unison, start, in measured augmentation, the first hexachord of the inverted series, at bar 231.

The voices, meanwhile, starting with the two soloists in rhythmic (though not melodic) canon at bar 227, develop a full canonic polyphony, arriving at rhythmic unison with the soloists for the culmination of the final 'Alleluia'.

One of the chief results of Stravinsky's use of serialism was his discovery of a new form of choral polyphony, based on canon. There is no doubt that the creative impulse behind this was religious; through choral music he rediscovered his religious nature. Moreover serialism was remote from subjective emotion, and he saw polyphony as the true music of the Church, the one which most truly reflected its spiritual aspiration. His new style is shown in its simplest and barest essentials in the short anthem *The Dove descending breaks the air*, which is a setting in four straightforward parts, without any deviation from a 3/4 metre, and without any transposition of the series from its fundamental position, of words from T. S. Eliot's 'Little Gidding'. Normally in short pieces, such as *Epitaphium*, *The Owl and the Pussy-cat*, Stravinsky uses the complete series untransposed, and avoids the complexity that comes with breaking up the hexachords.

The death of his friend T. S. Eliot on 4th January 1965 led to another short choral composition, this time in only two voice-parts—the single-movement *Introitus*, for male voices and a chamber ensemble of eight players, which is itself restricted to strings and percussion instruments of the 'male-voice' range. After the 'dramatic' choral works, Stravinsky here reverts to a more recognizably liturgical style. Tenors and basses intone the 'Introitus' from the Requiem—four melodic versions of the series, sung like a *cantus firmus*, interspersed with *parlando* sections. The reiterated notes that marked the *Elegy for J.F.K.*

reappear at bar 48 with the words 'et lux perpetua'; [1] numerous novelties of instrumentation include the complete series being given to the timpani, in the rhythm of 'requiem aeternam'.

The *Introitus*, in memory of a friend, was the prelude to his last choral work the following year, the *Requiem Canticles*. This is a very concise work, not liturgically complete; it was not intended for use at a funeral service, but rather as a 'monumentum spirituale'; it contains not lyricism but ritual. In this respect it differs from the Mass, though the two works have certain similarities; for instance, the choral homophony of 'exaudi', interspersed with instrumental interludes, recalls the *Agnus Dei* of the earlier work; also the melodic shape of the second series of the *Requiem Canticles* suggests the melody of the *Sanctus* of the Mass.

The first series of the *Requiem Canticles* has features in common with that of the *Introitus*: the prominence of fourths and fifths, for instance; but the later work is unique in that it uses two series. The necessity for the second was discovered at an early stage of the composition.

The *Requiem Canticles* is largely instrumental; short sections from the Latin Requiem are set within a three-fold instrumental framework, consisting of a Prelude for strings, an Interlude for wind instruments, a Postlude mainly for tuned percussion. All three are constructed round a repeated refrain. The symmetrical construction is given on page 128.

As he had already set the words 'requiem aeternam' in the *Introitus*, Stravinsky takes only a short part of the opening sentences ('exaudi orationem meam') to introduce two stanzas of the *Dies irae*. Each choral section of the work uses the voices in a different way; the first is homophonic, the next (*Dies irae*) uses a pitchless parlando, which is balanced in its turn by the final section ('libera me') in which Stravinsky combines *parlando*

---

[1] And again in the *Requiem Canticles* at bars 67, and 216–19.

Bars		Scoring
1–54	Instrumental Prelude Series I	
55–80	Exaudi	Chorus (cantabile, homophonic)
81–102	Dies irae	Chorus (cantabile, homophonic, parlando)
103–35	Tuba mirum	Bass solo
136–202	Instrumental Interlude Series II	
203–28	Rex tremendae	Chorus (cantabile, polyphonic)
229–65	Lacrimosa	Contralto solo
266–88	Libera me	Chorus (soli, cantabile, homophonic, parlando)
289–305	Instrumental postlude	

with *cantando* for four solo chorus voices, on rhythmically articulated chords.

The only choral polyphony ('Rex tremendae') occurs at the centre, after the Interlude: at this point Stravinsky introduces the second series, which is then sung in its entirety by sopranos and contraltos in unison (bars 216–21). The reiterated notes of this series are reminiscent of the *Elegy for J.F.K.*; they first appear in the Interlude at bar 169—the central, instrumental part of the work, which is the formal lament. The Postlude is the coda, in which the hexachords are chordally transformed, one set stationary, another moving in counterpoint, like a peal of bells. Robert Craft has it thus: 'The chord of Death, followed by silence, the tolling of bells, and again silence, all thrice repeated, then the three final chords of Death alone.'

16 Stravinsky's music: style and idea

Constant fresh discovery and renewal of the *materia musica* were what chiefly caused Stravinsky to exert such an influence over four generations of his contemporaries. No sooner, indeed, had the generation of the 'jazz age' comprehended some of the rhythmic implications of *Le Sacre* or *Histoire du soldat*, and acquired a taste, which they proceeded to indulge, for 'wrong notes', polytonality or displaced accents, than their originator was already leading off into the uncharted, tangential territory of neoclassicism.

That a new twentieth-century music could rest on, or evolve from, an old eighteenth-century or classical foundation, was an idea which many modernists found unacceptable; but for many others during the inter-war years it provided the necessary counterweight in Western music to the twelve-note technique, which was just beginning to emanate from Schoenberg and his circle. Thus the musical art became polarized; the mainstream of music had no longer a commonly accepted goal.

In time, Stravinsky's search for new sources from which to draw inspiration extended further into the past; Machaut and Gesualdo came to replace Bach and Beethoven. Once again he found himself the pace-setter for a considerable army of camp-followers among the post-1945 generation, who suddenly found that they too had a yen for mediaevalism—whether for texts of unintelligible meaning, or for pre-classical techniques, such as hocket and isorhythm.

Finally, by this time it is hardly surprising to note that the rising generation of the serial 60s should in their turn seize on his later works, as they embarked on an orgy of parameters, hexachordal rotations and 'combinatorial sets'. For them it was *Threni* or *Movements* which represented the real Stravinsky, the Stravinsky they could analyse, the newest and most authentic model Stravinsky, whose previous works were now superseded.

Such was the mesmeric hold that this composer had over European musicians. To each succeeding generation he displayed a different facet; with each succeeding work he altered the face of his music. Therefore his whole output, the total sum of his creativity, forms a steadily progressing unity, to which each work makes a distinctive, varied, unique contribution. From the multifarious variety of different musical sources and traditions, which he witnessed all around him, he selected only that material which could be unified, which he could then call his own. Once chosen, the musical idea was subject to his very clear and precise aesthetic discipline. 'I cannot compose,' he said, 'until I have determined what problems I must solve.'

As far as Stravinsky's choice and technical treatment of material are concerned, his *melos*, the foundation of his music, contains two basic patterns, which recur so frequently that they may be considered as inherent to his very nature.

The first pattern is a sequence of juxtaposed fourths. Clearly it is likely that this may have had its origin in Stravinsky's early awareness of folk-idioms; but the pattern runs through the full range of his works, from *The Firebird* to the *Requiem Canticles*. It appears in perhaps its most basic form in the little song, *Tilimbom*, from *Trois histoires pour enfants*:

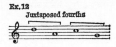

Ex. 12
Juxtaposed fourths

A familiar early example also occurs at the end of *The Firebird*:

The melodic lines of *Le Sacre* are also constructed on this popular basis; the horn at fig. 25, the trumpets at fig. 28+4, the strings at fig. 47, the flute at fig. 56+2, the violas at fig. 91, and the whole of the section up to fig. 97, are but a few examples. The melodic material of *Les Noces* is mostly constructed on the same basis.

From the enormous range of the middle period, examples may be cited from a dramatic work, *Persephone* (the flute solo for Persephone's final speech at fig. 250), and from an instrumental work (the theme of the third movement of the *Danses Concertantes*, starting at fig. 64). Perhaps the clearest example is the harp music at the opening of *Orpheus*, which recurs again at the apotheosis, at fig. 143:

The *Mass* too contains numerous examples of its use, for instance the oboe solos at the opening of the *Gloria*, or more particularly the vocal polyphony at the opening of the concluding *Agnus Dei*:

The melodic lines of the serial works also embody the same pattern; the recurring phrase in *De elegia prima* of *Threni* is a striking example (bars 42, 88, 142):

Numerous other instances might be quoted from that work, notably the leading tenor in Diphona I (bar 66).

In the *Variations* there is an interesting modification of the pattern as applied within the context of a serial composition. In the main section of the work, the eleven-bar phrase (starting at 23), thrice repeated, it is frequently suggested by the inter-

133

vallic writing. The series itself contains in its first hexachord the two adjacent fourths.

The second recurring pattern is made up of closely grouped semitones. One of the chief examples of the thematic use of this pattern, in an early work, is the five-note trombone solo in the *Danse sacrale* of the *Rite of Spring*:

Ex. 17

The chromatic inflection of a semitone is frequently used to colour an otherwise simple, diatonic harmony; often it leads to the simultaneous sounding of major and minor tonality, which is a very frequent characteristic; but this second basic pattern, recurring as it does through all his various phases, is more integral to Stravinsky's melodic style than such mere colouring might imply. The opening of *The Firebird* is a clear presentation of its use in an early work. The opening of the *Cantilène* of the *Duo Concertant*, to take a later instance, juxtaposes B and C thematically, not merely chromatically; this is picked up by the C–C♯, A–B♭ of the violin:

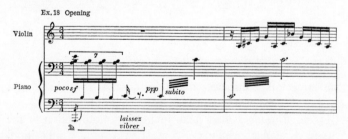

Ex. 18 Opening

The score of *Oedipus Rex* is another that is rich in examples of its use. The descending phrase at fig. 8, 'Theba moritur', recalled later in Oedipus' solo after fig. 45, summarizes the tragic theme of the story; the melodic line after fig. 83, which in turn recalls that at fig. 16, is a further example; above all, Jocasta's outburst, at the beginning of Act II, is built primarily round the pattern:

Ex.19

Jocasta: Nonn' e - ru - be - ski - te in— ae-gra ur - be cla - ma - re

In a less lugubrious context it occurs in the *Valse* in *Jeu de cartes*, for instance at fig. 143; also in the ensuring *Presto*, at fig. 163, and in several other points in that score. Also in the *Danses Concertantes*, which in some ways springs from *Jeu de cartes*, there are numerous instances of its thematic use; one occurs at fig. 153.

An interesting example of its use, which gives an impression of representing the essence of Stravinsky, and is highly reminiscent of the opening of *The Firebird*, occurs at the beginning of *Babel*. This work is constructed like a free passacaglia, with the sections in the form of variations on this bass:

Ex.20 Opening
Vc.,B.

p legato   etc.

That most poignant of ballets, *Orpheus*, makes extensive use of it; particularly at the entry of the oboes in Orpheus' *Air de danse*, and throughout the *pas de deux* for Orpheus and Eurydice. This music pleased Stravinsky. Indeed it seems possible that those parts of his work particularly pleased him which incorporate one or other of these basic melodic patterns.

Serialism by its nature lends itself to semitonal harmony; but the origin of Stravinsky's melodic use of this interval in the later works clearly lies also in this second basic pattern. The melodic shape of 'Surge aquilo', from the *Canticum Sacrum*, traces its descent directly from the examples already given:

Similarly the reliance on, and thematic importance given to, the interval of the semitone in *Movements* is no less, though the contexts differ, than the importance given to it in the *Mass*. In *Movements* the prominence given to the semitone results from the nature of the series, which consists of the second pattern, in different groupings; in the *Mass* the prominence given to the semitone results from the use of the Phrygian mode (for instance at fig. 46—2); but the melodic results are not dissimilar.

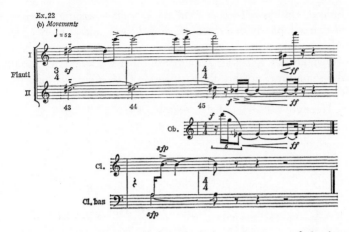

In one sense, some of Stravinsky's series are a bringing together, at the final stage of his life, of these two underlying melodic elements, fourths and semitones, which had been at the fountain of all his composition. This had happened before. One motif in particular was a fusion of the fourth pattern and the semitone pattern,[1] and it is noticeable that this very motif occurs as the chief thematic element of two of the most important works of Stravinsky's central period, the *Symphony of Psalms* and the *Symphony in C*:

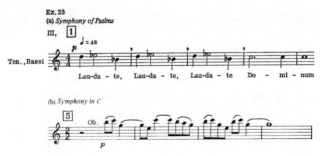

[1] See p. 94.

137

Indeed, this *Symphony in C* motif, so called because it occurs in that symphony in a more developed form, and as more of an inherent and primary feature than in any other work, has been shown already to colour a number of other works written round the same time, notably the *Dumbarton Oaks Concerto*,[1] and the *Concerto in D* for strings:

Here are the series of the serial works:

Ex. 24

[1] The phrase starting at fig. 10—1.

11 *Elegy for J. F. K.*

12 *Variations for Orchestra*

13 *Introitus*

14 *Requiem Canticles* (i)

Requiem Canticles (ii)

15 *The Owl and the Pussy-cat*

That sense of order which governed Stravinsky's whole life and work was apparent also in each individual composition. His choice of material, structure, instrumentation, tonality were equally important in the imposition of this order, both within each work, and between one work and the next, as his output progressively enlarged. In his studied avoidance of the ordinary, the expected, the cliché, he never repeated himself; each work is unique.

The harmonic and rhythmic means whereby he achieved this would require a volume to themselves for their adequate study. Frequently a scheme of related tonalities, or metrical inter-connection between one section and the next, are used to unify a composition; and to effect variety and change Stravinsky invented countless new forms of harmonic and metrical modulation. From a neoclassical work an example occurs in the *Gigue* of the *Duo Concertant*, where both harmonic and metrical modulation are effected simultaneously: A flat major modulates to A major, 9/16 modulates to 2/4 (see Ex. 25 overleaf).

From a serial work an example may be seen in *Abraham and Isaac*, in which the pace of the music changes and the narrative

of the drama thereby quickens, by Stravinsky's device of turning the pulse-unit of one phrase (in this case the semiquaver) into the metrical unit of the next:

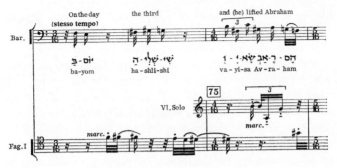

He had a sense of the material long before beginning to set it down on paper. The choice of instrumental ensemble, which would provide exactly the right individual sonority consistent with the overall purpose of a composition, often took a long time. *Les Noces* is one example of such a process; it was many years before the final decision was taken for the unusual ensemble of four pianos and percussion; the gamelan-like sonorities of the instruments had to be subservient to the voices, without betraying the percussive, peasant-like nature of the material. He wrote several different versions, whose common feature was that they all included keyboard instruments in the ensemble. He scored the first tableau with an orchestra the size of *Le Sacre*; then he tried groups of instruments with pianolas; another version was for woodwind and brass (including his favourite flügelhorn, which appeared much later in *Threni*), and with the cimbalom, which he used also in *Renard* and *Ragtime*; yet another version used two cimbaloms.[1]

Structure and instrumentation alike need to be congruent with the material if full unity is to be achieved. For instance, the succession of short movements which make up *Histoire du soldat* match its ragtime-band orchestration; while the three-

---

[1] These versions were played at the 1969 Berlin Festival (see J. Leach, *Composer* 40, Summer 1971).

fold instrumental framework of the totally different *Requiem Canticles* encloses the vocal sections of that work like a triptych —which in turn suggests further theological significance.

The coda-apotheosis, so marked a feature of many works, does not introduce fresh material. It started in the theatre, with *Petrushka*, and was later applied in purely instrumental or choral works. Moreover, between *Petrushka* and the *Requiem Canticles* Stravinsky introduced a new concept of tonality, through the use and disposition of instruments. He used not just pitch to determine tonality, but the quality of sound of the instruments, their timbre, and their relation with other instruments; also such keys to structure as symmetry and repetition. Tonality for him was an all-inclusive concept.

Ever since *The Firebird* he was precise in his use of instruments. Orchestral sonorities were the result of his trusting only his ear, while the characteristic clarity and dryness of articulation were essential to the realization of the rhythm. Nothing was left to chance; even a *fermata* is precisely notated in *Petrushka*, while the pianist is directed to play *f*, *secco*, using only the left pedal, and with the lid open.

Melodically, the repetition of short motifs, of small interval-span, is very common in works up to *Les Noces*. Rhythmically, Stravinsky constructs periods of equal and unequal rhythms. Phrases are broken up into shorter rhythmic units, which are in turn also underlined by the harmony and the instrumental texture. Variety is obtained by the addition of small-value notes to an otherwise regular metrical pattern. The incisive rhythms of *Le Sacre* are partly due to the requirements of choreography; they are certainly in total distinction to the style of the Impressionist composers, who tended to disguise the rhythm beneath a haze of orchestral tissue.

The development of purely instrumental structures following the *Octet* led Stravinsky to write longer periods, to re-think his use of the orchestra, to attend to the character of each instrument in a particular context. In the *Octet* he uses the wind instruments in pairs, according to their *timbre*; in the *Piano Concerto*, which totally avoids all reference to any Romantic orchestral associations, he uses material idiomatically, according to the characteristic nature of a particular instrument. The instrumentation of the *Symphony of Psalms* is highly individual. The enlarged wind and brass, but without clarinets, the absence of violins and violas, and the use of boys' voices, combine to create a sonority that is at one with the austere, ritualistic material.

Stravinsky's choice and use of instruments would properly form a separate study on their own. While other composers, Ravel for instance, might be highly skilled orchestrators, Stravinsky's invention is rooted in the very spirit of the instruments he uses. He makes particularly characteristic use, among many others, of the bassoon, the cor anglais, the oboe, the harp; of the trombone as a solo instrument in the *Symphony in C*, of the sarrusophone in *Threni*. He considered instruments, as Nabokov has remarked, as individuals.

As far as the use and disposition of the orchestra are concerned a turning-point is marked by the *Symphony in three movements*. Already in *Pulcinella* Stravinsky had divided the strings into *concertino* and *ripieno* sections, taking his cue from the eighteenth century; he also used wind instruments in groups. But with the *Symphony in three movements* he introduced a chamber-music flavour into the symphony. *Concertini*-groups of instruments are set against the wider ensemble, beginning with the development of the first movement at fig. 38. In the corresponding middle section of the slow movement, starting at fig. 125, instruments are used in solo.

Stravinsky's adoption of serialism after 1953 chiefly served to accentuate this trend. Where in earlier works the *tutti* had been built up from the bass line according to accepted principles of harmony, the characteristic sonority of his post-Webern works came from the contrapuntal interlocking and elaboration of separate strands of tone, largely for solo instruments or voices. The score is therefore linear, not full; moreover since most of the works of the later period are for voices, the use of the orchestra is, as a rule, sparing, if not secondary.

The work which provides the link to his later orchestral style is *Agon*. Again the instruments are divided into contrasted groups, according to pitch and timbre; moreover the brass are associated with the male dancers, the strings with the female dancers. As in the symphony, piano and harp are an integral part of the orchestra—as they will be from now on. The same process of reorganization of the orchestra continues with *Threni*; different groups are used in different vocal contexts. For instance, the choral canons of the *Querimonia* are placed with an instrumental chorus of three trombones.

The scoring of *A Sermon, a Narrative and a Prayer* consists of polyphonic solo parts; the orchestra is used very sparingly as a result, with no full passages. Moreover, the score itself is printed in a novel way, with the instruments grouped together according to pitch and timbre, and not according to the conventional grouping by categories. A short orchestral *tutti* occurs in *Movements* (137–40); a much longer one occurs in *The Flood*, for the storm sequence (399–456). In both cases Stravinsky uses the violins as one line, without dividing them into firsts and seconds. In *The Flood* he describes this effect of all the violins and flutes in unison as 'the skin drawn over the body of the sound'.

As he says, with reference to the *Variations*, 'the use of families and individuals in contrast is a principal projective element of the form [i.e. variation form] especially of its symmetries and reversibles'. Every since *The Firebird* innovation of timbre had pleased Stravinsky; in this case a variation for twelve solo violins, playing *ponticello*, proved both novel and consistent with his use of orchestral groupings. Elsewhere in the work the twelve violins play in unison.

If Stravinsky's early works tended to develop particularly his instrumental style, his vocal style evolved in the songs, and in such major works as *Renard* and *Les Noces*. That he already considered the voices as a sound-group, forming part of one undivided ensemble, is shown by his placing them with the instruments in these two works, as well as in *Pulcinella*. Moreover one innovation runs like a thread all through Stravinsky's vocal works. The male-duet idea, which first appears in *Le Rossignol* between the Chamberlain and the Bonze, was used frequently in later works of all periods, such as *Renard, Oedipus Rex, Threni*. In *The Flood* it is used for God's voice.

Other such constructional principles, already mentioned, which cover the whole range of his output and lend for consistency to his style, of whatever period, are the grouping of instruments according to sonorities, and a fondness for the use of variations as a unifying structure; indeed the two are not unconnected.

17 Stravinsky's aesthetic

Philosophy, according to Aristotle, begins in wonder. In the case of Stravinsky his wide-ranging, speculative wondering about the musical art led him to a complex, yet precise and logical aesthetic, which was partly a philosophy, the product of his intellect, and partly a discipline, the product of his creativity. Indeed the one flowed from the other; the only laws that he obeyed in composition were those that he detected and identified as part of the true nature of music. He, more than any other twentieth-century composer, rediscovered and reformulated the basic nature of the *materia musica*, which had become obscured by various disorderly, anarchical developments in composition, originating in the later nineteenth century. Of these, the pursuit of nationalistic folklore, academicism and post-Wagnerian decadence were the chief.

Stravinsky's aesthetic, his speculative concepts, encompassed nothing less than a world-view, and a certain spiritual standard of living, as much as principles of art. They were based on a never-ceasing search for order and unity, out of the chaos and disunity that were everywhere apparent. The desire to create, and to compose, was part of his being; but it was not of itself enough to ensure such unity. It needed to be restrained and disciplined if it were to become truly productive. Whereas the artisan-musician of the Middle Ages was subject automatically to an imposed social discipline, the artist-musician of the post-Renaissance, and particularly since the Romantic period, needs to make his own aesthetic rules.

Composition, the organization of sound and time—the two basic elements of music—is a conscious human act. Creativity therefore begins with a free, speculative volition on the part of the composer; a 'willing' to bring a conception within the order of his aesthetic. Writing down is thus inseparable from creation; 'inspiration', in the Romantic sense of the word, is chronologically secondary.

Achieving order and unity over the element of sound means discovering the appropriate measure of subordination of the disorder of dissonance to the security of consonance; more broadly, curbing a 'Dionysian' self-assertiveness with an 'Apollonian' restraint. Although strongly clashing tone-colours produce an immediate and violent sensation, this is only effective against a more stable background. Achieving order and unity over the element of time means discovering the relationship between variable rhythms and invariable metres; between the contrasts of the music's progress, as measured by its tempo and tone, and the regularity of ontological time, as measured by a clock. Irregularity is only effective when set against regularity. It was precisely Webern's 'in-depth' solution of the time-factor of music that so appealed to Stravinsky.

In both elements, sound and time, the listener needs a point of reference, or sameness, against which the specific requirements of the composer, or diversity, are set.

Such an objective view of music led Stravinsky to devote long years of the central period of his life to a search for such abstract, autonomous structures of instrumental music as would satisfy him. The climax was reached with the two great symphonies. But to some extent this twentieth-century reinstatement by him of classical principles originated in the ballets, and in the direct link between gesture and tone. As he says of *Les Noces*; 'the sight of the gesture and movement of the different parts of the body that produce the music are essential to seizing it in all its breadth.' Not that he set out in the ballet scores to

147

'explain' the action; on the contrary, all bodily movements, such as the action and choreography, arose out of the music, which was self-sufficient. Balanchine always started with the music, which he set about 'visualizing'. As Stravinsky once said, he attempted to 'make visible not only the rhythm, melody and harmony, but even the *timbres* of the instruments'.

Stravinsky's objective aesthetic was the very opposite to that of the Romantics. Whereas bodily rhythms and movements might be related afterwards to his musical rhythms and movements, the nineteenth-century Romantics took emotions as their models beforehand for musical expression. Stravinsky was by no means indifferent to human emotion, but he mistrusted such a subjective basis for the taxing process of human creativity. Music for him could only exist objectively; it could not 'express' subjectively. Therefore it achieves its highest point, its purest forms, in absolute structures, not in any subservient role. An early example may be cited from the history of church music, in which, starting from monody, which was the means adopted for clear intonation of the words, mediaeval musicians developed the absolute structures of polyphony—Masses and motets—which attained levels of pure art far beyond the reach of monody.

The nineteenth-century conception of a 'synthesis of the arts' was false; Wagner's music-drama wreaked all the havoc of a decadent period. Wagnerism represented, in theological language, the 'fall' of Western music; that point in its evolution when individual creative insubordination, and questioning of integrating order, became artistically acceptable; even, as time went by, necessary. Gone were those accepted values that had given music both continuity and a common language, and that had enabled composers to rise to universal greatness, like beacons of light. Instead, 'music lost its melodic smile'. Paradise was lost.

The twentieth century was the heir to that situation. Indeed, the dichotomy between Schoenberg's and Stravinsky's aesthetic may be measured in their response to it. Schoenberg continued, and spelt out, the implications, as he saw them, of the Wagnerian choice, which he accepted as part of the inevitable evolution of German music. Stravinsky, on the other hand, resought those principles of order, in a wider sense, that Wagner had cast aside; he reasserted the human creative will against the destructive power of uncontrolled, order-less caprice, and the anarchy of apparently infinite freedom. Paradoxically his aesthetic rests on the assumption, which is a Christian principle, that in the acceptance of constraints, the human creative spirit becomes free. As Leonardo da Vinci said, 'strength is born of constraint, and dies in freedom'.

Stravinsky's aesthetic evolved as his perspectives changed. He was strongly aware, from the start, of the strength of that conscious, corporate culture, otherwise called tradition, into which he was born. National traditions are the soil from which spring the composers whose music is international. As he put it, 'tradition is carried forward in order to produce something new'. *Mavra* is a clear example of this process.

The Russian tradition in which Stravinsky grew up consisted of several interlocking layers: first, 'The Five'—those successors of Glinka and Dargomijsky, whose aesthetic was based on a popularization of folklore; second, the group round Belaiev, including Glazunov, who were chiefly noted for a certain academicism; next, the lonely and somewhat ambiguous figure of Scriabin; finally, and greatest of all, Tchaikovsky.

But it was not long before Stravinsky's creativity outgrew the soil of the Russian tradition, as he gravitated westwards. That was the first real moment in which he asserted that 'speculative volition' which, as he has shown, is also the first necessity for any other twentieth-century composer who is not merely to drift on the tide of those historical events to which he is the heir. If the *melos* of such works as *Histoire du soldat* and *Les Noces* was innate in his Russian origin, that of later works, of the neo-classical and serial periods, was more the result of choice, consciously and deliberately made; more 'artificial', in the true sense of the word.

His curiosity was matched by his possessive instinct: 'Everything that fascinates me, everything I love, I seek to make mine. I suffer, no doubt, a special sort of kleptomania.' The past was just as much a living reality for him as the present; and the discovery of a sense of style was central to his creativity. Thus 'back', in the historical sense of 'back to Bach', did not mean 'backwards' in the aesthetic sense of 'reactionary'. Musical speculation could be exercised on any primary material whatever, whether that of Josquin, Pergolesi or Webern. Stravinsky took an established method or technique—jazz, eighteenth-century formalism, folklore, serialism—and considered whether it had a place in his work, whether he could make it his own.

The use of models is something common to every young composer; but what most do at the apprentice stage, for want of experience, Stravinsky was to do in his maturity, as a matter of choice and of artistic necessity. He took not merely a work, or a style, but a whole cultural tradition. Why should he not take possession of the twentieth-century Viennese tradition that Webern represented? Could he, indeed, afford not to?

Stravinsky and Schoenberg were at opposite aesthetic poles. For Stravinsky, atonalism was chaos; moreover he had no time for the dogmatism of Schoenberg's Draconian twelve-note laws. 'Schoenberg,' he said, 'is as far from my aesthetic as can be.' The contrast between the two [1] is indeed total, and symptomatic of their differing solutions to the twentieth-century situation. Schoenberg was concerned with theory, Stravinsky with practice. Schoenberg dogmatized, Stravinsky speculated.

[1] See *Dialogues and a Diary*, pp. 107–9.

Schoenberg taught, and rarely performed; Stravinsky performed, and rarely taught. Schoenberg was a nationalist, Stravinsky a cosmopolitan. Schoenberg was an introvert, Stravinsky an extrovert. One of the few things that they shared, except disciples, was a mutual antipathy.

But Schoenberg's pupil Webern was very different. Unlike Berg, who had compromised with them, Webern interpreted the twelve-note laws of his teacher; and his interpretation resulted in serialism—which seemed to Stravinsky to hold out the possibility of greatly enlarging the perspective of the musical language. The Webern songs, for instance, introduced to him an 'entirely new concept of order'. So serialism seemed not so much a dogma to be obeyed, as a creative principle to be interpreted.

Over a period of sixty years, when it seemed that Western music, in the wake of Wagner, faced disintegration and decay, or at very least radical modification, as one experiment succeeded another, and composers brooded, analysed or dogmatized, Stravinsky rose above the mêlée. He reimposed standards of universal primacy for the art, at a time when they were being whittled away. He reasserted the possibility of greatness in music, at a time when the trend of contemporary thought was to question, or deny, the validity of any such concept. In an age of widespread cynicism, atheism and clever-clever parody, he dared to offer his music in praise of God; and with it he sought to 'represent Paradise and become the bride of the Cosmos'. He confronted a society which laid chief store by technological advance, with the piercing logic of his aesthetic. He countered scepticism with certainty. In an age of non-commitment, aleatoricism, improvisation, he was committed, disciplined and precise.

Because each piece is different, and none is derivative, there are no 'major' and 'minor' categories in Stravinsky's output. *Apollo* is polyphonic, *Persephone* homophonic; *Le Sacre* uses a huge orchestra, *Histoire du soldat* a very small one; *Threni* is triadic, *Movements* is not; *The Rake's Progress* lasts two and a half hours, *Epitaphium* lasts one and a quarter minutes. All are equally part of the total output; each has its own, unique, aesthetic *raison d'être*.

Appendix A   Calendar

Figures in brackets denote the age reached by the person mentioned during the year in question.

YEAR	AGE	LIFE	CONTEMPORARY MUSICIANS

1882 — Igor Fedorovich Stravinsky born, June 18, at Oranienbaum outside St Petersburg, of Polish ancestry, son of Feodor Ignatievich, bass singer at the opera house, and his wife Anna.

Kodály born, Dec. 16; Malipiero born, Mar. 18; Szymanowski born, Oct. 6; Arensky 20; Balakirev 45; Bartók 1; Belaiev 46; Bloch 1; Borodin 49; Brahms 49; Bruckner 58; Busoni 16; Chabrier 41; Chausson 27; Cui 47; Diaghilev 10; Debussy 20; Delage 2; Delibes 46; Delius 20; d'Indy 31; Dukas 17; Duparc 34; Dvořák 41; Elgar 25; Falla 5; Fauré 37; Glazunov 17; Gounod 64; Grieg 39; Ives 7; Janacek 27; Koussevitzky 7; Liadov 27; Mahler 22; Medtner 2; Miaskovsky 1; Puccini 24; Rakhmaninov 9; Ravel 7; Rebikov 16; Rimsky-Korsakov 38; Roslavetz 1; Roussel 13; Rubinstein 52; Ruggles 6; Satie 16; (Florent) Schmitt 11; Schoenberg 8; Scriabin 10; Sibe-

YEAR	AGE	LIFE	CONTEMPORARY MUSICIANS
			lius 16; Smetana 58; Strauss 18; Sullivan 40; (Serge) Taneiev 26; Tchaikovsky 42; (Nicholas) Tcherepnin 9; Vaughan Williams 10; Verdi 69; Wolf 22.
1883	1		Casella born, July 25; Gnessin born, Feb. 2; Webern born, Dec. 3.
1884	2		Smetana (60) dies, May 12.
1885	3		Berg born, Feb. 9; Riegger born, Apr. 29; Varèse born, Dec. 22; Wellesz born, Oct. 21.
1886	4		
1887	5		Borodin (53) dies, Feb. 27.
1888	6		Durey born, May 27.
1889	7		
1890	8	First sees *The Sleeping Beauty*	Martin born, Sep. 15; Martinů born, Dec. 8.
1891	9	Meets Catherine Nossenko. Visits Frankfurt, hears *Die Fledermaus* and *Zigeunerbaron*. First piano lessons.	Bliss born, Aug. 2; Delibes (55) dies, Jan. 16; Prokofiev born, April 23.
1892	10	Summer at Pechisky. Fair at Yarmolintsy impresses him.	Honegger born, March 10; Milhaud born, Sept. 4.
1893	11	Assists at first opera performance, Glinka's *A Life for the Tsar*.	Gounod (75) dies, Oct. 18; Tchaikovsky (53) dies, Nov. 6.
1894	12		Chabrier (53) dies, Sept. 13; Piston born, Jan. 20; Rubinstein (65) dies, Nov. 20.
1895	13	Ill with pleurisy and tuberculosis. Holiday at Interlaken.	Hindemith born, Nov. 16.

YEAR	AGE	LIFE	CONTEMPORARY MUSICIANS
1896	14		Bruckner (72) dies, Oct. 11; Gerhard born, Sept. 25; Sessions born, Dec. 28.
1897	15		Brahms (64) dies, April 3; Tansman born, June 12.
1898	16		Gershwin born, Sept. 25.
1899	17		Auric born, Feb. 15; Chausson (44) dies, June 10; Chavez born, June 13; Poulenc born, Jan. 7; Tcherepnin born, Jan. 21.
1900	18	Studies counterpoint by himself (instinctive aversion to study of harmony); also Russian and French music, and Wagner.	Antheil born, July 8; Barraud born, April 23; Copland born, Nov. 14; Křenek born, Aug. 23; Sullivan (58) dies, Nov. 22; Weill born, March 2.
1901	19	Enters St Petersburg University to study law. Meets Rimsky-Korsakov (summer).	Sauguet born, May 18; Verdi (88) dies, Jan. 27.
1902	20	Seeks advice from Rimsky-Korsakov, who agrees to teach him, privately, orchestration and form. Father dies, Dec. 4.	Walton born, March 29.
1903	21		Blacher born, Jan. 3; Khachaturian born, June 6; Nabokov born, April 17; Wolf (43) dies, Feb. 22.
1904	22		Belaiev (67) dies, Jan. 10; Dallapiccola born, Feb. 3; Dvořák (63) dies, May 1; Kabalevsky born, Dec. 30; Petrassi born, July 16; Skalkottas born, March 8.

YEAR	AGE	LIFE	CONTEMPORARY MUSICIANS
1905	23	*Piano Sonata in F sharp minor* played, Feb. 9. Degree in jurisprudence at University. Holiday in Scandinavia with Goury, May. *Symphony in E flat* started.	Jolivet born, Aug. 8; Lambert born, Aug. 23; Rawsthorne born, May 2; Tippett born, Jan. 2.
1906	24	*The Faun and the Shepherdess.* Marries his cousin, Catherine Nossenko, Jan. 24.	Arensky (44) dies, Feb. 25; Finney born, Dec. 23; Shostakovich born, Sep. 25.
1907	25	*Symphony in E flat* performed, April 27, *Pastorale.* Son Theodore born.	Fortner born, Oct. 12; Grieg (64) dies, Sept. 4.
1908	26	Begins first sketch of *The Nightingale: Four Studies* for piano. Gorodetzky songs performed (winter). Daughter Ludmilla (Mika) born.	Carter born, Dec. 11; Lesur born, Nov. 19; Messiaen born, Dec. 10; Rimsky-Korsakov (64) dies, June 21.
1909	27	*Fireworks* and *Scherzo Fantastique,* 6 Feb., impresses Diaghilev, whose Russian Ballet was first seen in Paris. Commissioned to write *The Firebird.*	
1910	28	*The Firebird* first performed in Paris, June 25. Sees Debussy's *Pelléas et Mélisande. Rite of Spring* first conceived; consults Nicholas Roerich about Slavonic mythology. Summer in Brittany; *Two poems of Verlaine. Petrushka* started. Son Soulima born, Sept. 23.	Balakirev (74) dies, May 30; Barber born, March 9.

YEAR	AGE	LIFE	CONTEMPORARY MUSICIANS
1911	29	Ill with nicotine poisoning. *Petrushka* first performed in Paris, June 13. *Two poems, Zvezdoliki* (Balmont). Meets Ansermet. Starts *Rite of Spring*.	Mahler (51) dies, May 18; Ussachevsky born, Nov. 3.
1912	30	Hears *Parsifal* at Bayreuth with Diaghilev. Scandal of Nijinsky's *L'après midi d'un Faune*. Visits Budapest, London, Vienna with *Ballets Russes*. Meets Schoenberg in Berlin, hears *Pierrot Lunaire*, Dec. 8.	Cage born, Sept. 15; Françaix born, May 23; Martinet born, Nov. 8.
1913	31	*Three Japanese Lyrics. Rite of Spring* first performed in Paris, May 29. Ill with typhoid. Convalesces in Oustilug. Settles at Clarens, in Switzerland.	Britten born, Nov. 22; Khrennikov born, June 10.
1914	32	Daughter Maria Milena born, Feb. *The Nightingale* first performed in Paris, May 26. *Rite of Spring* performed in concert version. Returns to Clarens; begins *Les Noces*. Visits Russia (July), collects poems of Kirievsky and Afanasiev. *Pribaoutki, Three pieces for String Quartet*. Outbreak of war. Visits Diaghilev in Florence.	Liadov (59) dies, Aug. 28; Panufnik born, Sept. 24.
1915	33	Visits Diaghilev in Rome. Meets Ramuz. Begins *Renard*; moves to Morges.	Palmer born, June 2; Scriabin (43) dies, April 27; (Serge) Taneiev (59) dies

YEAR	AGE	LIFE	CONTEMPORARY MUSICIANS
		Conducts for the first time in Geneva (Dec.).	June 19.
1916	34	*Ballets Russes* sail for America, Jan. 1. Sees Princess de Polignac; completes *Renard, Berceuses du chat.* Goes to Madrid to meet Diaghilev, May 26. Ill with neuralgia (Dec.).	ApIvor born, April 14; Babbitt born, May 10.
1917	35	*Les Noces* (short score) finished. *Four Russian Peasant Songs.* Visits Diaghilev in Rome (March); hears *The Good-humoured Ladies,* to Scarlatti's music. First ideas for *Histoire du soldat.* Satie's *Parade* performed in Paris. Brother Goury dies on Roumanian front. October Revolution in Russia.	
1918	36	*Histoire du soldat* first performed in Lausanne, Sept. 28. *Ragtime* finished at the moment of armistice, at 11.00, Nov. 11.	Cui (83) dies, March 24; Debussy (55) dies, March 25.
1919	37	*Four Russian Songs.* Visits Diaghilev in Paris; *Pulcinella* suggested. *Piano-Rag-Music,* Nov. 8.	
1920	38	Leaves Switzerland, moves to France. *Pulcinella* first performed in Paris, May 15. *Concertino for String Quartet. Symphonies of wind instruments.*	Rebikov (54) dies, Dec. 1.
1921	39	Visits Spain. Conducts	

YEAR	AGE	LIFE	CONTEMPORARY MUSICIANS
		Petrushka in Madrid. Tour of Belgium, Holland, Switzerland, Germany. *Symphonies of wind instruments* first performed in London, June 10. Meets Vera de Bosset, July 14. *The Sleeping Beauty*, Nov. 21.	
1922	40	*Renard,* May 18; *Mavra,* June 3; his mother emigrates from Russia.	Xenakis born, May 29.
1923	41	*Les Noces* first performed in Paris, June 13; *Octet,* Oct. 13; Visits Monte Carlo, Weimar; meets Busoni.	
1924	42	Debut as pianist in *Piano Concerto,* May 22. Concert tour. *Piano Sonata.* Settles at Nice. Children ill with diphtheria.	Busoni (58) dies, July 27; Fauré (79) dies, Nov. 4; Nigg born, June 6; Nono born, Jan. 29; Puccini (66) dies, Nov. 29.
1925	43	Tour of U.S.A., Europe. *Serenade* for Piano. Plays *Sonata* at Donaueschingen, Venice. *Oedipus Rex* planned with Cocteau.	Berio born, Oct. 24; Philippot born, Feb. 2; Satie (59) dies, July 1; Schuller born, Nov. 22.
1926	44	European concert tour. Conducts *Le Rossignol,* *Petrushka* at La Scala, Milan.	Henze born, July 1.
1927	45	*Oedipus Rex* first performed in Paris, May 30. *Apollo* commissioned.	
1928	46	*Apollo* first performed in Washington, April 27; in	Barraqué born, Jan. 17; Janáček (74) dies, Aug. 12;

YEAR	AGE	LIFE	CONTEMPORARY MUSICIANS
		Paris, June 12. *The Fairy's Kiss* first performed in Paris, Nov. 27.	Stockhausen born, Aug. 22.
1929	47	European concert tour. Plays first performance of *Capriccio*, Dec. 6.	Diaghilev (57) dies, Aug. 19; Pousseur born, June 23.
1930	48	Plays and conducts in European tours. *Four Studies for Orchestra* first performed in Berlin, Nov. 7. *Symphony of Psalms* first performed in Brussels, Dec. 13.	
1931	49	Moves to Voreppe, near Grenoble. Meets violinist Dushkin. *Violin Concerto* first performed in Berlin, Oct. 23.	d'Indy (80) dies Dec. 1.
1932	50	*Duo Concertant* first performed in Berlin, Oct. 28. European concert tour with Dushkin.	
1933	51	Meets Gide at Wiesbaden. *Persephone* begun. Soulima makes début in *Capriccio*, in Barcelona. Hitler's rise to power; Schoenberg leaves Germany.	Duparc (85) dies, Feb. 12; Penderecki born, Nov. 25.
1934	52	*Persephone* first performed in Paris, April 30. Concert tour with Dushkin. Becomes French citizen, June 10. Moves to Paris.	Davies born, Sept. 8; Delius (72) dies, June 10; Elgar (76) dies, Feb. 23.
1935	53	Second tour of U.S.A.: visits Hollywood. Applies unsuccessfully for *Institut*	Berg dies (50), Dec. 24; Dukas (69) dies, May 17.

YEAR	AGE	LIFE	CONTEMPORARY MUSICIANS
		de France. Concerto for two pianos first performed in Paris, with Soulima, Nov. 21, followed by tour of South America. *Chroniques de ma vie* published.	
1936	54	Tour of Europe and South America with Soulima. *Jeu de cartes* commissioned.	Amy born, Aug. 29; Glazunov (70) dies Mar. 21.
1937	55	Third tour of U.S.A. Conducts first performance of *Jeu de cartes* in New York, April 27. *Concerto, 'Dumbarton Oaks'* begun.	Gershwin (38) dies, July 11; Ravel (62) dies, Dec. 28; Roussel (68) dies, Aug. 23; Szymanowski (54) dies, March 29.
1938	56	*Concerto, 'Dumbarton Oaks'* first performed in Washington, May 8. Begins *Symphony in C.* Munich crisis. Daughter Ludmilla dies, Nov. 30.	
1939	57	*Zvezdoliki* first performed in Brussels, April 19. Wife dies, March 2; mother dies, June 7. Ill for five months. *Poetics of Music.* Outbreak of Second World War. Lands in America Sept. 30. Lectures at Harvard.	
1940	58	Marries Vera de Bosset, March 9. Settles in California. *Symphony in C* first performed in Chicago, Nov. 7.	
1941	59	*Danses Concertantes.*	
1942	60	*Danses Concertantes* first performed in Los Angeles,	

YEAR	AGE	LIFE	CONTEMPORARY MUSICIANS
		Feb. 8. *Circus Polka; Four Norwegian Moods.* Natalie Koussevitzky dies. Begins *Symphony in three movements.*	
1943	61	*Ode* first performed in Boston, Oct. 8; Begins *Sonata for two pianos.*	Rakhmaninov (69) dies, March 28.
1944	62	*Scènes de Ballet, Scherzo à la Russe, Babel, Elegy. Sonata for two pianos* first performed.	
1945	63	*Symphony in three movements* completed. End of Second World War. Becomes American citizen, Dec. 28.	Bartók (64) dies, Sept. 26; Tcherepnin (72) dies, June 26; Webern (61) dies, Sept. 15.
1946	64	Conducts first performance of *Symphony in three movements,* in New York, Jan. 24. *Basle Concerto* written.	Falla (89) dies, Nov. 14.
1947	65	*Basle Concerto* first performed, Jan. 27. *Orpheus* written. *Mass.* Daughter Maria Milena, with her husband, moves to California. Meets W. H. Auden (Nov.).	Casella (63) dies, March 5.
1948	66	Meets Robert Craft, March 31. Begins Act I of *The Rake's Progress. Orpheus* first performed in New York, April 28. *Mass* first performed in Milan, Oct. 27.	
1949	67	*The Rake's Progress,* Act II.	Skalkottas (45) dies, Sept.

YEAR	AGE	LIFE	CONTEMPORARY MUSICIANS
		Conducts concerts on tour of America.	20; Strauss (85) dies, Sept. 8.
1950	68	*The Rake's Progress*, Act. III. Conducts concerts on tour of America.	Miaskovsky (69) dies, Aug. 8; Weill (50) dies, April 3.
1951	69	European tour, Aug.–Nov. Conducts *The Rake's Progress* at first performance in Venice, Sept. 11, and further concerts.	Koussevitzky (75) dies, June 4; Lambert (45) dies, Aug. 21; Medtner (71) dies, Nov. 13; Schoenberg (77) dies, July 13.
1952	70	European tour, April–June. Studies serialism, particularly Webern. Begins *Septet* (July). Directs first performance of *Cantata* in Los Angeles, Nov. 11.	
1953	71	Concerts, recordings. Finishes *Septet*, begins *Three Shakespeare songs*. Discusses proposed opera with Dylan Thomas, May 22. Dylan Thomas dies, Nov. 9.	Prokofiev (61) dies, March 4.
1954	72	*Septet* first performed at Dumbarton Oaks, Jan. 23. *Three Shakespeare songs* first performed, March 8. European tour, April–June. *In memoriam Dylan Thomas* first performed, Sept. 20.	Ives (79) dies, May 19.
1955	73	Concerts in America. European tour March–May. Writes *Canticum Sacrum*.	Honegger (63) dies, Nov. 27.
1956	74	*Canonic Variations* (Bach) first performed, May 27. European tour, June–Dec.	

YEAR	AGE	LIFE	CONTEMPORARY MUSICIANS
		Conducts first performance of *Canticum Sacrum* in Venice, Sept. 13.	
1957	75	Concerts in America. First concert performance of *Agon* in Los Angeles at a 75th birthday concert, June 17. European tour, Aug.–Oct. Begins *Threni*.	Gnessin (74) dies, May 5; Sibelius (91) dies, Sept. 20.
1958	76	Concerts in America. European tour, July–Dec. Conducts first performance of *Threni* in Venice, Sept. 23. Audience with Pope John, Nov. 26. Begins *Movements*.	Vaughan Williams (86) dies, Aug. 26; Schmitt (88) dies, Aug. 17.
1959	77	*Double Canon for String Quartet.* Japanese tour, March–May. Receives Sonning Prize, Copenhagen (May). European tour, Sept.–Nov. Concerts and recordings in New York. Publishes first book of conversations with Robert Craft (see Appendix D).	Antheil (58) dies, Feb. 12; Bloch (78) dies, July 15; Martinů (68) dies, Aug. 28.
1960	78	Concerts and recordings. *Movements* first performed in New York, Jan. 10. Italian tour, Sept.–Dec. Conducts first performance of *Monumentum pro Gesualdo* in Venice, Sept. 27. Begins *A Sermon, a Narrative and a Prayer*.	

YEAR	AGE	LIFE	CONTEMPORARY MUSICIANS
1961	79	Concerts and recordings. Visit from Russian composers (June 8), who invite him to visit the U.S.S.R. the following year. Begins *The Flood.* European tour, Sept.–Dec., also includes Egypt and the Pacific.	Delage (81) dies, Sept. 21; Riegger (75) dies, April 2.
1962	80	Dinner at the White House with President and Mrs Kennedy, Jan. 18. *A Sermon, a Narrative and a Prayer* first performed Basel, Feb. 23. *The Flood* recorded for television, March 26–8. *Eight instrumental miniatures* first performed in Los Angeles, March 26. European tour, May–June. 80th birthday concert in Hamburg, June 18. Concerts in America, July. Tour to include Israel, U.S.S.R. Aug.–Oct. Begins *Abraham and Isaac.*	
1963	81	European tour, April–June. Hears Monteux conduct *Rite of Spring* in London, May 29, the 50th anniversary of première. President Kennedy assassinated, Aldous Huxley dies, Nov. 22. Tour of Italy, Nov. Begins *Variations for Orchestra.*	Poulenc (64) dies, Jan. 31.
1964	82	Concerts and recordings.	

YEAR	AGE	LIFE	CONTEMPORARY MUSICIANS
		Elegy for J.F.K. first performed in Los Angeles, April 6. Visit to Israel. *Abraham and Isaac* first performed in Jerusalem, Aug. 23. Completes *Variations for Orchestra*.	
1965	83	T. S. Eliot dies, Jan 4. *Variations for Orchestra* first performed in Chicago, April 17. Also *Introitus*, at same concert. Visits Poland, May –June; decorated by Pope Paul at a concert in the Vatican, June 12. Visits London, last concert, Sept. 14. Begins *Requiem Canticles*.	Varèse (80) dies, Nov. 6.
1966	84	*Requiem Canticles* first performed at Princeton, Oct. 8. *The Owl and the Pussy Cat* first performed in Los Angeles, Oct. 31. European tour, May–June. Begins piano work, Dec.	
1967	85	Conducts for last time (*Pulcinella* in Toronto, May 17). Records for last time (*The Firebird*, Jan. 18). Ill in hospital, Aug.–Sept.	Kodály (84) dies, March 6.
1968	86	Transcribes Wolf songs. Attends concerts in America. Wolf transcriptions first performed in Los Angeles, Sept. 6. Visits Zürich, Paris, Sept.–Nov.	

YEAR	AGE	LIFE
1969	87	Ill in New York, May–June. Transcribes Bach Preludes and Fugues. Moves from Hollywood to New York, Sept. 14.
1970	88	Ill in hospital, April. Visits Europe, stays at Evian, June–Aug.
1971	89	Begins composing 'an idea beginning with a combination of *tierces*', March 3. Last illness, March 18; dies April 6. Buried at Venice, on the island of San Michele, April 15.

CONTEMPORARY MUSICIANS

Gerhard (73) dies, Jan. 10.

Amy 34; ApIvor 54; Auric 72; Babbitt 51; Barber 61; Barraqué 43; Barraud 70; Berio 45; Blacher 68; Bliss 79; Britten 57; Cage 58; Carter 62; Chavez 71; Copland 70; Dallapiccola 67; Davies 37; Finney 64; Fortner 63; Françaix 58; Henze 44; Jolivet 65; Kabalevsky 66; Khatchaturian 67; Křenek 70; Khrennikov 57; Lesur 62; Martin 81; Martinet 59; Messiaen 64; Milhaud 62; Nabokov 67; Nigg 46; Nono 47; Palmer 55; Panufnik 56; Penderecki 45; Petrassi 66; Philippot 46; Piston 77; Pousseur 41; Rawsthorne 65; Sauguet 69; Schuller 45; Sessions 74; Shostakovich 64; Stockhausen 42; Tippett 66; Ussachevsky 59; Walton 69; Wellesz 85; Xenakis 48.

Appendix B   Catalogue of works

I. BALLETS, OPERAS, MUSICAL AND DRAMATIC WORKS
(Concert suites taken from stage works are listed under VIb.)

L'Oiseau de feu—The Firebird (Ballet in two tableaux)   1909–10
Pétrouchka—Petrushka (Burlesque in four tableaux)   1910–11
                                                       (rev. 1946–7)
Le Sacre du printemps—The Rite of Spring (Scenes of   1911–13
    Pagan Russia in two parts)   (rev. 1921, 1943)
Le Rossignol—The Nightingale (Lyric Tale in three acts)   1908–14
                                                       (rev. 1962)
Renard—Reynard (A Burlesque in song and dance)   1915–16
Histoire du soldat—The Soldier's Tale (To be read,
    played and danced, in three parts)   1918
Pulcinella (Ballet in one act)   1919–20
Mavra (Opera in one act)   1921–2
Les Noces—The Wedding (Russian dance scenes with
    song and music)   1914–23
Oedipus Rex (Opera-Oratorio in two acts)   1926–7
                                                       (rev. 1948)
Apollon Musagète—Apollo Musagetes (Ballet in two   1927–8
    tableaux)   (rev. 1947)
Le Baiser de la Fée—The Fairy's Kiss (Ballet in four   1928
    scenes)   (rev. 1950)
Persephone (Melodrama in three tableaux)   1933–4
                                                       (rev. 1949)
Jeu de cartes—The Card Party (Ballet in three deals)   1936
Orphée—Orpheus (Ballet in three scenes)   1947

The Rake's Progress (Opera in three acts)	1948–51
Agon (Ballet for twelve dancers)	1953–7
The Flood (A musical play)	1961–2

II. ORCHESTRAL WORKS, CONCERTOS, WORKS FOR JAZZ GROUPS

Symphony in E flat	1905–7
Scherzo Fantastique	1907–8
Feu d'artifice—Fireworks (Orchestral Fantasy)	1908
Ragtime (i) version for eleven instruments (ii) version for piano solo	1918
Symphonies of wind instruments	1920
	(rev. 1945–7)
Concerto for piano and wind instruments (i) full version	1923–4
(ii) version for two pianos	(rev. 1950)
Capriccio for piano and orchestra	1928–9
	(rev. 1949)
Violin Concerto	1931
Concerto in E flat for 15 instruments ('Dumbarton Oaks')	1937–8
Symphony in C	1938–40
Danses Concertantes for 24 instruments	1941–2
Circus Polka (for a young elephant) (i) version for wind and percussion (ii) version for full orchestra (iii) version for piano solo	1942
Four Norwegian Moods	1942
Ode (Elegiacal Chant in three parts)	1943
Scherzo à la Russe (i) version for jazz band (ii) version for full orchestra	1943–4
Scènes de Ballet	1944
Symphony in three movements	1942–5
Ebony Concerto, for jazz band	1945
Concerto in D for Strings ('Basle')	1946
Greeting Prelude	1955
Movements for piano and orchestra	1958–9
Variations for orchestra (Aldous Huxley in memoriam)	1963–4

III. CANTATAS AND CHORAL WORKS

Zvezdoliki—*Le roi des étoiles* (Balmont) for male-voice choir and orchestra	1911–12
Four Russian Peasant Songs ('Soucoupes—Saucers') for unaccompanied female choir	1914–17
On Saints' Days in Chigisakh	
Ovsen	
The Pike	
Master Portly	
Pater noster, for unaccompanied choir	1926
	(rev. 1949)
Symphonie de Psaumes—Symphony of Psalms, for children's and mixed voices, and orchestra	1930 (rev. 1948)
Credo, for unaccompanied choir	1932
	(rev. 1949, 1964)
Ave Maria, for unaccompanied choir	1934
	(rev. 1949)
Babel (Cantata), for male chorus, narrator and orchestra	1944
Mass, for mixed chorus and double wind quintet	1944–8
Cantata, for soprano, tenor, female chorus and five instruments	1951–2
Canticum Sacrum, for tenor, baritone, mixed chorus and orchestra	1955
Threni: id est lamentationes Jeremiae Prophetae for 6 soli, mixed chorus and orchestra	1957–8
A Sermon, a Narrative and a Prayer (Cantata) for contralto, tenor, speaker, chorus and orchestra	1960–1
Anthem—'The Dove descending breaks the Air' (T. S. Eliot) for unaccompanied choir	1962
Introitus (T. S. Eliot in memoriam) for male chorus and 8 instruments	1965
Requiem Canticles for contralto and bass soli, chorus and orchestra	1965–6

IV. SONGS FOR SOLO VOICE

(with piano, instrumental, orchestral accompaniment)

Le Faune et la bergère—The Faun and the Shepherdess (Pushkin) for voice and orchestra	1906
La Bergére	
Le Faune	
Le Torrent	
Pastorale (wordless vocalise) for voice and piano	1907
Two melodies (Gorodetzky) for voice and piano	1907–8
Chanson de printemps	
La rosée sainte	
Two poems of Verlaine, for voice and piano	1910
Un grand sommeil noir	
La lune blanche	
Two poems of Balmont, for voice and piano	1911
Fleurette—The Flower	
Le Pigeon—The Dove	
Three Japanese Lyrics	1913
(i) version for soprano and piano (ii) version for soprano and small orchestra	
Akahito	
Mazatsumi	
Tsaraiuki	
Souvenirs de mon enfance—Recollections of my childhood Three little songs for voice and piano, dedicated to his children	1906–13
La Petite pie—The Magpie	
Le Corbeau—The Rook	
Tchitcher—Iatcher—The Jackdaw	
Pribaoutki—Chansons plaisantes, for voice and 8 instruments	1914
L'oncle Armand—Kornillo	
Le Four—Natashka	
Le Colonel—The Colonel	
Le Vieux et le lièvre—The old man and the hare	

Berceuses du chat—Cat's cradle songs, for voice and three
    clarinets   1915–16
        Sur le poêle
        Intérieur
        Dodo
        Ce qu'il a le chat
Trois histoires pour enfants—Three stories for children,
    for voice and piano   1915–17
        Tilimbom
        Les Canards (Ducks), *Les Cygnes* (Swans)
        Les Oies (Geese)
        Chanson de l'ours (Song of the Bear)
Berceuse, for voice and piano   1917
Four Russian songs, for voice and piano   1918–19
        Canard
        Chanson pour compter
        Le Moineau est assis
        Chant dissident
Three songs from William Shakespeare, for voice, flute,
    clarinet and viola   1953
        Musick to heare   (*Eighth sonnet*)
        Full Fadom Five   (*The Tempest*)
        When Daisies pied   (*Love's Labour's Lost*)
In memoriam Dylan Thomas, for tenor, string quartet, four
    trombones   1954
Abraham and Isaac (sacred ballad) for baritone and
    orchestra   1962–3
Elegy for J.F.K. (W. H. Auden), for baritone (or mezzo-
    soprano) and 3 clarinets   1964
The Owl and the Pussy-cat (Edward Lear), for voice
    and piano   1966

V. PIANO AND CHAMBER MUSIC

Four Studies for piano	1908
Three pieces for string quartet	1914
Three easy pieces for piano duet (see also under VI)	1914–15

    March
    Waltz
    Polka

Souvenir d'une Marche Boche for piano	1915
Five easy pieces for piano duet (see also under VI)	1916–17

    Andante
    Española
    Balalaika
    Napolitana
    Galop

Valse pour les enfants	1917
Study for pianola ('Madrid')	1917
Piano-Rag-Music, for piano solo	1919
Three pieces for solo clarinet	1919
Concertino for string quartet (see also under VI)	1920
Les cinq doigts. Eight easy pieces for piano (see also under VI)	1920–1
Octet for wind instruments	1922–3 (rev. 1952)
Sonata for piano	1924
Serenade in A for piano	1925
Duo Concertant, for violin and piano	1931–2
Concerto for two solo pianos	1931–5
Tango for piano solo (see also under VI)	1940
Sonata for two pianos	1943–4
Elegy for unaccompanied viola	1944
(i) version for viola (ii) version for violin (a fifth higher)	
Septet for clarinet, horn, bassoon, piano, string trio	1952–3
Epitaphium, for flute, clarinet, harp	1959
Double canon, Raoul Dufy in memoriam, for string quartet	1959

VI. ARRANGEMENTS, ORCHESTRATIONS, ADAPTATIONS, TRANSCRIPTIONS

(by Stravinsky only; excluding arrangements of Stravinsky's work by others)

A. OTHER COMPOSERS' WORKS

Nocturne in A flat, Valse brillante in E flat (Chopin)— orchestration	1909
Kobold (Grieg)—orchestration	
Song of the flea (Beethoven) ⎫—orchestration	1909
Song of the flea (Mussorgsky) ⎭	1910
Khovanshchina (Mussorgsky)—finale arranged and orchestrated	1913
Chant des bateliers du Volga—Song of the Volga boatmen arranged for wind and percussion, under the title *Hymne à la nouvelle Russie*	1917
The Sleeping Beauty (Tchaikovsky)—orchestration	1921
The Sleeping Beauty (Tchaikovsky)	1941
The Bluebird, Pas de deux (Act III) arranged for small orchestra	
The Star-spangled Banner, arranged and orchestrated	1941
Canonic Variations (J. S. Bach) on the carol *Vom Himmel hoch*, arranged for mixed chorus and orchestra	1955–6
Tres Cantiones Sacrae (Gesualdo) completed, recomposed	1957–9
Da pacem Domine	
Assumpta est Maria	
Illumina nos	
Monumentum pro Gesualdo. Three madrigals (Gesualdo) recomposed for instruments.	1960
Asciugate i begli occhi	
Ma tu, cagion di quella	
Beltà poi che t'assenti	
Canzonetta for strings (Sibelius, Op. 62a) arranged for 8 instruments	1963

Two sacred songs from the 'Spanisches Liederbuch' (Hugo
   Wolf) transcribed for voice and 10 instruments   1968
      Herr, was trägt der Boden hier
      Wunden trägst du . . .

B. STRAVINSKY'S OWN WORKS

(i) Adaptations and arrangements of stage works for concert use

STAGE WORK		CONCERT WORK	
The Firebird	1	Orchestral Suite, *The Firebird*	1911, 1919, 1945
	2	*Prélude et Ronde des Princesses,* for violin and piano	1929
	3	*Berceuse,* for violin and piano	1929, 1933
	4	*Scherzo,* for violin and piano	1933
	5	Canon for orchestra	1965
Petrushka	1	Three movements for piano solo	1921
	2	*Danse Russe*—Russian Dance, for violin and piano	1932
Le Rossignol	1	*Chant du Rossignol*—Symphonic Poem	1917
	2	*Air de Rossignol, Marche Chinoise,* for violin and piano	1932
Histoire du soldat	1	Suite, arranged for violin, clarinet and piano	1919
	2	Instrumental suite, in 8 movements	1920
Pulcinella	1	Orchestral suite, in 8 movements	1919–22 (rev. 1949)
	2	Suite for violin and piano	1925
	3	*Suite Italienne,* for violoncello and piano	1932
	4	*Suite Italienne,* for violin and piano	1933
Mavra	1	*Chanson Russe*—Russian song, for violin and piano	1937
	2	*Chanson Russe*—Russian song, for violoncello and piano	1937
The Fairy's Kiss	1	*Divertimento,* for violin and piano	1932

Stravinsky

STAGE WORK	CONCERT WORK	
	2 *Divertimento*, for orchestra	1934 (rev. 1949)
	3 *Ballad*, for violin and piano	1934, 1947
The Rake's Progress	*Lullaby*, recomposed for two recorders, descant and treble	1960

(ii) Adaptations and arrangements of songs and chamber music

ORIGINAL WORK	ADAPTATION	
Pastorale	1 Transcribed for soprano, oboe, cor anglais, clarinet, bassoon	1923
	2 Lengthened version for violin and piano	1933
	3 Lengthened version for violin and 4 wind instruments	1933
Two poems of Verlaine	Rescored for voice and small orchestra	1910, 1914, 1951
Two poems of Balmont	Rescored for voice and small orchestra	1954
Souvenirs de mon enfance	Rescored for voice and small orchestra	1929–30
Three pieces for string quartet	1 *Quatre études—Four studies* for orchestra	1914–28 (rev. 1952)
Étude for pianola	2 *Étude* transcribed for two pianos (by Soulima Stravinsky)	1951
Four Russian peasant songs ('*Soucoupes —Saucers*')	Rescored for female voices and four horns	1954
Eight easy pieces for piano duet	1 *Polka* transcribed for cimbalom	1915
	2 Suites Nos. 1 and 2 for small orchestra	1917–25
	Suite No. 1 *Andante* *Napolitana* *Española* *Balalaika*	

ORIGINAL WORK	ADAPTATION		
	Suite No. 2	*Marche*	*Valse*
		Polka	*Galop*
Trois histoires pour enfants	1 *Tilimbom* rescored for voice and orchestra		1923
	2 *Tilimbom, Geese, Swans,* rescored for voice, flute, harp, guitar		1954
Tango	1 First instrumental version		1941
	2 Second instrumental version		1953
Four Russian Songs	*The Drake, A Russian spiritual* rescored for voice, flute, harp, guitar		1953–4
Concertino for string quartet	Rescored as *Concertino for 12 instruments*		1952
Les cinq doigts	Rescored as *Eight Instrumental Miniatures* for 15 players		1962

VII. MISCELLANEOUS, EARLY OR UNPUBLISHED WORKS

Scherzo for piano	1902
Storm Cloud, for voice and piano	1902
Plaisanteries musicales	1903
Piano Sonata in F sharp minor	1903–4
The mushroom going to war, for bass voice and piano	1904
Cantata (unnamed)	1904
Conductor in Tarantula, for piano	1906
Chant funèbre for wind instruments in memory of Rimsky-Korsakov	1908
Canons for two horns	1917
Duet for two bassoons	1918
Praeludium for jazz ensemble	1936
ii version for piano (by Soulima Stravinsky); iii rescored 1953	
Petit Ramusianum Harmonique, for unaccompanied voice	1937

Stravinsky

Little canon for two tenors   1947
Cinq pièces monométriques, for instrumental ensemble
    (incomplete)   1920–1
Fanfare for a new theatre for, two trumpets   1964
Instrumentation of four preludes and fugues, from
    The Well-Tempered Clavier (J. S. Bach)   1969

Appendix C   Personalia

Ansermet, Ernest (1883–1969), Swiss conductor; formerly professor of mathematics at Lausanne. Founded Orchestre de la Suisse Romande (1918). Much admired by Stravinsky, but later severely criticized by him, following unauthorized cuts in *Apollo* and *Jeu de cartes*. Author of musico-mathematical treatise *Les fondements de la Musique* (1961) against serialism.

Auberjonois, René-Victor (1872–1948), Swiss painter, designer of sets and costumes for *Histoire du soldat*. Friend of Ramuz (q.v.).

Auden, Wystan Hugh (1907–73), English poet, playwright, editor, lecturer. Associated with Isherwood (q.v.) and others in authorship of plays. Professor of poetry, Oxford University (1956–61). Librettist, with Chester Kallman, of *The Rake's Progress*.

Babin, Victor (1908–72), Russian pianist, particularly noted for two-piano arrangements (e.g. *Circus Polka*) which he played with his wife Vitya Vronsky (q.v.).

Bakst, Léon (1866–1924), Russian painter, designer. Associated with Diaghilev.

Balanchine (Balanchivadƶe), George (1904–), born St Petersburg. Father and brother composers. Choreographer; first with Diaghilev, later in Copenhagen, Monte Carlo, New York, where he founded School of American Ballet (1934). Director of New York City Ballet since 1948.

Balmont, Konstantin Dmitryevich (1867–1943), Russian Symbolist poet. Stravinsky set his *Zveƶdoliki*.

Benois, Alexandre Nikolaevich (1870–1960), Russian painter, of Italian, French and German extraction. Associated with Diaghilev. Designed sets and costumes of *Petrushka*.

Berlin, Sir Isaiah (1909–), lecturer in philosophy, Oxford, since 1932. Professor of social and political theory (1957–67). Visiting lecturer to various American universities.

Berman, Eugene (1899–), Russian painter, lived in California (1940). Designer for *Danses Concertantes*.

Berners, Lord (Gerald Hugh Tyrwhitt-Wilson) (1883–1950), English composer and eccentric.

Bernstein, Leonard (1918–), American conductor, pianist, lecturer. Composer of popular musicals, musical comedies, etc. (e.g. *West Side Story*).

Bliss, Mr and Mrs Robert Woods, wealthy American patrons of music, and owners of estate at Dumbarton Oaks, Georgetown, D.C. Commissioned Stravinsky's *Concerto in E flat*, and *Symphony in C*.

Bolm, Adolph Rudolphovich (1890–1958), Russian dancer, choreographer of *Apollo*.

Boulanger, Nadia (1887–), French teacher, conductor, composer. Director of American Conservatory of Music, Fontainebleau (1949).

Boulez, Pierre (1925–), French *avant-garde* composer, conductor, writer. Pupil of Messiaen. For their analysis of Stravinsky's *Le Sacre*, see Appendix D, Section B.

Chagall, Marc (1887–), Russian artist; Surrealist. Lived in France (1922), America (1941), France (1948).

Chirico, Giorgio de (1888–), Italian artist; associated with the Surrealists (1925); described his work as 'metaphysical painting'.

Cingria, Charles-Albert (1883–1954), Swiss writer, friend of Stravinsky.

Cocteau, Jean (1889–1962), French writer, poet, critic, playwright, film-maker and wit. Sponsor of numerous *avant-garde* movements; associated with *Les Six*.

Craft, Robert (1924–), American conductor, writer. Friend and companion of Stravinsky since 1948, and collaborator with him in published *Conversations* (see Appendix D, Section B.)

Dahl, Ingolf (1912–70), American composer, pianist, conductor, of Swedish descent. Lecturer at University of South California after 1945, specifically on Stravinsky. Associated with 'Evenings on the roof' concerts in Los Angeles. Friend and colleague of Stravinsky, translated 'Poétique Musicale'.

Delaunay, Robert (1885–1941), French artist, founder of *Orphism*.

Dolin, Anton (*Patrick Healey-Kay*) (1904–), British dancer, choreographer. Associated with Diaghilev from 1921; later formed company with Markova (q.v.). Founded London Festival Ballet (1950).

Dufy, Raoul (1877–1953), French artist, designer.

Dushkin, Samuel (1896–), American violinist of Russian birth. As well as introducing Stravinsky's *Violin Concerto* and *Duo*, he was the dedicatee of new works by other composers, such as Ravel, Prokofiev and Pierné.

Eliot, Thomas Stearn (1888–1965), American poet, critic, resident in England, Nobel prizewinner.

Flonzaley Quartet. Founded in New York (1902) by a Swiss banker, De Coppet. Widely acclaimed for exceptional ensemble; disbanded in 1928. Stravinsky wrote the *Concertino* for them.

Fokine, Mikhail (1880–1942), Russian dancer, choreographer; created choreography for *The Firebird* and *Petrushka*.

Giacometti, Alberto (1901–66), Swiss sculptor and painter; worked in Paris; surrealist, abstract.

Gide, André Paul Guillaume (1869–1951), French writer, Nobel prizewinner. Works include fiction, poetry, drama, criticism, autobiography. Librettist of *Persephone*.

Golovine, Alexander (1863–1930), Russian painter. Designed sets and costumes for *The Firebird*.

Gorodetzky, Sergei (1885–1967), Russian poet, set by Stravinsky in some early songs. Later reacted against Symbolism (cf. Balmont).

Heard, [*Henry Fitz*]*Gerald* (1889–), English writer, lecturer, mystic, friend of Stravinsky. Associated with Huxley and Isherwood (q.v.) in the study of Eastern religions.

Stravinsky

Herman, Woody (1913–), American jazz musician, leader of several
bands (the Herman Herds, the Four Brothers). Of the première
of Stravinsky's *Ebony Concerto* in Carnegie Hall, 25th March
1946, Herman said: 'There never will be a night again like the
1946 Carnegie Hall concert. The band fulfilled itself that night.'

Horgan, Paul (1903–), American novelist, historian and lecturer.

Hurok, Sol (1888–), Russian-born American impresario.

Huxley, Aldous Leonard (1894–1963), English novelist, essayist.
Moved to California in 1937, where he and his first wife Maria
(d. 1955) became close friends of Stravinsky.

Isherwood, Christopher William (1904–), English novelist, playwright, associate and friend of W. H. Auden (q.v.). American
citizen (1946), Professor at University of California (1965).

Karsavina, Tamara (1885–), Russian dancer; created roles in *The
Firebird, Petrushka, Pulcinella*.

Khrennikov, Tikhon Nicolaievich (1913–), Russian traditional composer and teacher. Secretary General of the Union of Soviet
Composers (1948); First Secretary (1957).

Kirstein, Lincoln (1907–), American ballet producer. Director of
New York City Ballet.

Klemperer, Otto (1885–1973), German conductor, to start with chiefly
of opera.

Kochanski, Pawel (1887–1934), Polish violinist; taught both at St
Petersburg (1913) and New York (1924). Transcribed Stravinsky's *The Firebird* for violin, as well as works of other composers.

Kochno, Boris (1904–), Russian poet; Diaghilev's secretary. Wrote
verse libretto of *Mavra*.

Koussevitzky, Sergey Alexandrovich (1874–1951), bass player, conductor, publisher. Supporter and patron of numerous composers
by means of publication, commissions, and (later) awarding
prizes through the Koussevitzky Music Foundation, in memory
of his wife Natalie (d. 1941).

Křenek, Ernst (1900–), Austrian-born American composer, writer
and lecturer. Professor of Music at Vassar College, New York
(1939–42), and St Paul, Minnesota (1942–7).

Larionov, Mikhail Fedorovich (1881–1964), Russian painter; designer of *Renard,* and dedicatee of Stravinsky's *Berceuses du chat.*

Liebermann, Rolf (1910–), Swiss musician, Director of Hamburg State Opera (1959–72). Lived in Paris since 1973. Engaged in dispute with Boulez (q.v.) on the viability and the future of opera.

Lifar, Sergey (1905–), Russian dancer, choreographer. Associated with Diaghilev since 1923. Lived and worked in Paris, mainly at Paris Opéra. Wrote biography of Diaghilev (1940).

Lourié, Arthur Vincent (1892–), Russian composer, writer, theorist; resident in America since 1940.

MacNeice, Louis (1907–63), Belfast-born English poet, writer, critic.

Mann, Thomas (1875–1955), German novelist; mother a talented musician, brother also a novelist. Settled in America in 1936. His best-known work *Doktor Faustus* appeared in 1947.

Marinetti, Emilio Filippo Tommaso (1876–1944), Italian poet and writer, known for his anti-traditionalism, and 'futurism'.

Marion, André, Stravinsky's French-born son-in-law, married to his younger daughter Milena. He acted as Stravinsky's accountant and business manager, as well as working as a travel agent. A suit was filed against him (1969) by Stravinsky's attorney, Weissberger, for the recovery of manuscripts, and this resulted in estrangement.

Maritain, Jacques (1882–), French Catholic philosopher and theologian; writer on art and history.

Markova, Dame Alicia (Lilian Alicia Marks) (1910–), English ballerina, dancer in *Le Rossignol.* Collaborated with Dolin (q.v.). Appointments include Director of Metropolitan Opera Ballet of New York (1963–9).

Massine, Léonide (1896–), Russian-born American dancer and choreographer. Principal dancer with Diaghilev, and creator of choreography for *Le Sacre, Le Rossignol, Pulcinella.* Later with the Ballet Russe de Monte Carlo.

Matisse, Henri (1869–1954), French artist.

Milhaud, Darius (1892–1974), French composer, resident in America. Member of *Les Six* in the 1920s; Professor at Mills College, California (1940–7).

Monteux, Pierre (1875–1964), French conductor. Appointments included the Metropolitan Opera, New York (1917–19), Boston Symphony (1919–24).

Morton, Lawrence (1904–   ), American musician; keyboard player, arranger and composer for films. 1954–71, directed 'Monday Evening Concerts' in Los Angeles (formerly 'Evenings on the Roof'). Director Ojai Festivals 1954–9, and 1967–70. Since 1965 Curator of Music at Los Angeles County Museum of Art. Directed over 90 Stravinsky performances, including 14 premières (5 more than Diaghilev), and 2 all-Stravinsky concerts, on his 80th and 85th birthdays. *Eight Instrumental Miniatures* dedicated to him.

Nabokov, Nicholas (1903–   ), Russian-born American composer and writer. Friend and chronicler of Stravinsky (see Appendix D). His career has run parallel to that of Stravinsky: his ballet-oratorio was produced by Diaghilev; his works were heard in Venice Festivals; he wrote an opera to a W. H. Auden libretto; he lived in Paris and America. The main difference is that he is also a teacher, and has held a post in Baltimore, U.S.A., since 1947.

Nijinska, Bronislava (1891–   ), sister of Vaslav Nijinsky (q.v.). Russian dancer and choreographer, associated with Diaghilev. Created choreography for *Renard, Les Noces, The Fairy's Kiss, Mavra*.

Nijinsky, Vaslav (1890–1950), Russian dancer, associated with Diaghilev. Created role of *Petrushka*, choreography for *Le Sacre*. Later became insane.

Onnou, Alphonse (1893–1940), Belgian violinist; founder of the Pro Arte String Quartet (1913), which specialized in contemporary music.

Perse, St John (*Marie René Auguste Alexis Saint-Léger Léger*) (1887–   ), French poet and diplomat. Nobel prizewinner.

Picasso, Pablo (1881–1972), Andalusian-born painter and sculptor. Moved to Paris (1901). Dominant figure in French, and European, art, particularly known for 'cubism'. Associated with Diaghilev, and designed costumes and sets for *Pulcinella*.

Piovesan, Alessandro (1908–58), administrator and author. Director of Venice Biennale 1952–7. Commissioned Stravinsky's *Canticum Sacrum*. *Threni* was dedicated to his memory.

Polignac, Princess Edmond de (18?–1945), American heiress; patron and benefactress to composers; held notable Parisian *salon* since early 1900s. Commissioned Stravinsky's *Renard, Oedipus Rex*; previews in her house of *Les Noces, Piano Concerto, Persephone*. Stravinsky also dedicated the *Piano Sonata* to her.

Prévost, Germain (1891–), Belgian viola-player, member of the Pro Arte String Quartet (see under Onnou). Stravinsky wrote the *Elegy* for him.

Ramuz, Charles Ferdinand (1878–1947), Swiss writer, living in the Vaud canton. Collaborated with Stravinsky in translating Russian texts into French, such as *Histoire du soldat* (see Appendix D.

Respighi, Ottorino (1879–1936), Italian composer and violinist. Pupil of Rimsky-Korsakov.

Rimsky-Korsakov, Nikolai Andreievich (1844–1908), Russian composer, teacher of Stravinsky.

Roerich, Nicolas Konstantinovich (1874–1947), Russian painter, folklorist. Designed *Le Sacre*, which is dedicated to him.

Roland-Manuel, Alexis (1891–), French writer, critic and composer. Author of books on Ravel and Falla.

Rolland, Romain (1866–1944), French writer, novelist, playwright and musicologist. Professor of history of music in Paris (1910). Nobel prizewinner.

Rubinstein, Artur (1887–), Polish-born American pianist.

Rubinstein, Ida (1880–1960), wealthy Russian-Jewish dancer, promoter and patron. Commissioned Stravinsky's *The Fairy's Kiss* and *Persephone*.

Sacher, Paul (1906–), Swiss musician and conductor. Founded Basle Chamber Orchestra (1926), and other organizations. Commissioned Stravinsky's *Concerto in D*.

Shilkret, Nathaniel (1895–   ), American conductor and publisher, and originator of the joint oratorio *Genesis* (to which Stravinsky contributed *Babel*). Other composers involved were Schoenberg, Milhaud, Toch and Castlenuovo-Tedesco.

Siloti, Alexander (1863–1945), Russian pianist and conductor.

Souvtchinsky, Pierre (1892–   ), Russian-born philosopher, writer, and close lifelong friend of Stravinsky. Attended première of *Fireworks* (1908); founded *The Musical Contemporary* (1915); discussed *The Poetics of Music* with Stravinsky in 1939; founded 'Domaine Musical' concerts in Paris, with Boulez (q.v.). Author, editor ('Musique Russe', 1953). French citizen 1930. Consultant on Stravinsky archive project.

Spender, Stephen (1909–   ), English poet, critic and editor. Professor of English, in London (1970).

Spies, Claudio (1925–   ), American composer and writer. Professor of Music at Princeton (1970).

Steinberg, Maximilian Osseyevich (1883–1946), Russian composer and teacher. Son-in-law of Rimsky-Korsakov (q.v.).

Stokowski, Leopold Bołesławowicz Stanisław Antoni (1882–   ), American conductor; champion of many contemporary composers. Founded American Symphony Orchestra, New York (1962).

Tansman, Alexandre (1897–   ), Polish composer, resident in California (1940), French citizen (1937).

Tchelichev, Pavel (1898–   ), Russian artist; designed *Apollo*, and *Balustrade* (to Stravinsky's *Violin Concerto*).

Thomas, Dylan (1914–53), Welsh poet and writer. Planned an opera with Stravinsky.

Ussachevsky, Vladimir (1911–   ), Russian composer, resident in America. Noted for electronic compositions.

Valéry, Paul-Ambroise (1871–1945), French poet and writer.

Varèse, Edgard (1885–1965), French-born American composer, whose experimental works earned Stravinsky's approval; e.g. *Ionisation* (1931), for 35 percussion instruments, and *Déserts* (1954).

Vlad, Roman (1919–   ), Italian writer, composer and critic. (See
   Appendix D.)
Vronsky, Vitya, see under *Babin, Victor.*

Walter, Bruno (1876–1962), German-Austrian conductor, mainly
   known as a romantic interpreter, particularly of Mahler.
Waugh, Evelyn Arthur St John (1903–66), English novelist, satirist,
   eccentric.
Werfel, Franz (1890–1945), Austrian poet, dramatist and novelist.
   Lived in America since 1940.
Whiteman, Paul (1891–1967), American jazz musician and bandleader.
   Many pieces written for him included Gershwin's *Porgy and
   Bess.*

Yevtushenko, Yevgeny Alexandrovich (1933–   ), Russian poet, born
   in Siberia. Visited Stravinsky in California in December 1966.

Appendix D   Bibliography

A complete Stravinsky bibliography is beyond the scope of this book. The following select bibliography lists the essential literature and omits magazine articles, critical reviews and other Stravinskyana, which have already reached distended proportions. Existing lists include:

Hamilton, David, discography, compiled for the special memorial issue of *Perspectives of New Music*, 1971 (see C)

Magriel, Paul, bibliography of over 600 books and articles in *Stravinsky in the Theatre*, ed. Lederman (see B).

Wade, Carroll D., bibliography compiled for *Stravinsky: a new appraisal of his work*, ed. Lang (see C).

The following bibliography is divided into three sections:

A   Books by Stravinsky himself
B   First-hand accounts by those who knew him personally
C   Other books, and some works of general reference

A   BOOKS BY STRAVINSKY HIMSELF

Chroniques de ma vie, 2 vols. (Paris, 1935), trans. as *Chronicle of my life* (London, 1936); *An autobiography* (New York, 1936); *Cronicas de mi vida* (Buenos Aires, 1935–6); *Erinnerungen* (Zürich, 1937).

Poétique Musicale (Harvard, 1942), trans. as *Poetics of Music* (Harvard, 1947); *Musikalische Poetik* [1] (Mainz, 1949).

[1] Published in 1957 together with 'Antworten auf 35 Fragen' as Igor Strawinsky: Leben und Werk, von ihm selbst (Mainz)

188

WITH ROBERT CRAFT

Conversations with Igor Stravinsky (New York and London, 1959).
Memories and Commentaries (New York and London, 1960).
Expositions and Developments (New York and London, 1962).
Dialogues and a Diary (New York, 1963; London, 1968).[1]
Themes and Episodes (New York, 1966).
Retrospectives and Conclusions (New York, 1969).
Themes and Conclusions (London, 1972).

LETTERS

Igor Stravinsky: Documents and Materials (ed. and annotated by Igor
   Blazhkov (Moscow, 1973).
I. F. Stravinsky: Essays and Materials, compiled by L. S. D'yachkova,
   ed. B. M. Yarustovsky (Moscow, 1973).
F. Stravinsky: Essays, Letters, Memoirs (compiled and annotated by
   L. Kutateladze, ed. A. Gozenpud (Leningrad, 1972).

B FIRST-HAND ACCOUNTS OF STRAVINSKY OR HIS MUSIC BY THOSE WHO KNEW HIM PERSONALLY

Ansermet, Ernest, 'Stravinsky' and 'Note sur Stravinsky' in *Les
   fondements de la musique* (Neuchâtel, 1961). See also under
   Lederman.
Boulez, Pierre, 'Stravinsky demeure' in *Relevés d'apprenti* (Paris,
   1966). Reprinted from *Musique Russe*, ed Souvtchinsky (q.v.),
   1953.
Casella, Alfredo, *Igor Strawinsky* (Rome, 1926).
Craft, Robert, 'A Concert for St Mark' (*The Score,* Dec. 1956). 'A
   personal preface' (*The Score,* June 1957). 'Gesualdo and Stravinsky' (*Tempo* 45, Aug. 1957). 'Stravinsky's Russian Letters'
   (*New York Review,* Feb. 1974). 'The Rite of Spring' (*Perspectives,* 1966). See also under Corle and Lederman. *The Chronicle
   of a Friendship* (London, 1972). *Prejudices in disguise* (New
   York, 1974). 'Stravinsky in the twenties' (*New York Review,*

[1] Vols. 1–4 published in a Soviet edition (Leningrad, 1971).

2nd May 1974). With Piovesan, Alessandro, and Vlad, Roman: *Le Musiche religiose di Igor Strawinsky* (Venice, 1956).

Horgan, Paul, *Encounters with Stravinsky* (London, 1972).

Libman, Lillian, *And music at the close* (London, 1972).

Malipiero, G. F., *Strawinsky* (Venice, 1945).

Nabokov, Nicolas, *Igor Stravinsky* (Berlin, 1964). *Old friends and new music* (London, 1951). See also under Corle.

Ramuz, C. F., *Souvenirs sur Igor Stravinsky* (Lausanne, 1926).

Souvtchinsky, Pierre, *Igor Stravinsky* (Cologne, 1963). Requiem Canticles (*Tempo* 86, Autumn 1968).

Stravinsky, Theodore, *Le message d'Igor Strawinsky* (Lausanne, 1948), trans. as *Igor Strawinsky: Mensch und Künstler* (Mainz, 1952); *The message of Igor Stravinsky* (London, 1953). *Catherine and Igor Stravinsky—a family album* (London, 1973).

Tansman, Alexandre, *Igor Stravinsky* (Paris, 1948), trans. as *Igor Stravinsky, the man and his music* (London, 1949); *Igor Stravinsky* (Buenos Aires, 1949).

COMPOSITE PUBLICATIONS

Armitage, Merle (ed.), *Igor Stravinsky* (11 contributors) (New York, 1936).

Cahiers de Belgique (5 contributors) (Brussels, Dec. 1930).

Corle, Edwin (ed.), *Igor Stravinsky* (16 contributors) (New York, 1949).

La Revue Musicale (5 contributors) (Paris, Dec. 1923); (14 contributors) (Paris, May–June 1939).

Lederman, Minna (ed.), *Stravinsky in the theatre* (23 contributors) (New York, 1948; London, 1951).

C OTHER BOOKS, AND SOME WORKS OF GENERAL REFERENCE

Benois, Alexandre, *Reminiscences of the Russian Ballet* (London, 1941).

Fokine, M., *Fokine: Memoirs of a Ballet Master* (London, 1961).

Goldner, Nancy, *The Stravinsky Festival of the New York City Ballet* (New York, 1974).

Grigoriev, S. L., *The Diaghilev Ballet, 1909–1929* (London, 1953).

Lifar, Serge, *Diaghilev* (London, 1940).

Piovesan, Alessandro. See under Craft in Section B.

Siohan, Robert, *Stravinsky* (Paris, 1959; London, 1965).

Vlad, Roman, *Stravinsky*. See also under Craft in Section B. (Rome, 1958; London, 1960, 1967).

White, Eric Walter, *Stravinsky: the composer and his works* (London, 1966).

COMPOSITE PUBLICATIONS

Éditions de Réalités (Hachette). *Stravinsky* (8 contributors) (Paris, 1968).

Lang, Paul Henry (ed.), *Stravinsky: a new appraisal of his work* (7 contributors) (New York, 1963).

Perspectives of new music. Stravinsky: a composer's memorial (62 contributors) (1971).

WORKS OF GENERAL REFERENCE

Honegger, Marc (ed.), *Dictionnaire de la musique* (Paris, 1970).

Slonimsky, Nicholas, *Music since 1900* (4th ed. London, 1971).

Appendix E   Notes on the Stravinsky family

SUPPLIED BY THEODORE STRAVINSKY

p. 1 : Originally the Counts Soulima-Stravinsky resided in territories of Eastern Poland which were annexed by Catherine the Great. Their natural sentiments of patriotism could only displease the Empress, who, in order to minimize them, took away the title of 'Count' as well as the name 'Soulima'—leaving only the name Stravinsky.

p. 53 : Stravinsky's son Soulima, with his wife and son John, joined Stravinsky in Hollywood in 1948; and stayed there until he became professor at the School of Music of the University of Illinois. He kept seeing his father as often as his professional activities permitted.

Stravinsky's eldest son Theodore and his wife lived, and still live, in Geneva. He never missed an opportunity to visit his father during Stravinsky's trips to Europe, and flew over twice to America when he learned about his father's illness. During the last summer at Evian (1970) he saw him daily.

Index

Index

Afanasiev, Alexander, 16, 17, 21, 77
Andersen, Hans, 35
Ansermet, Ernest, 16, 17, 18, 21, 23, 25, 27, 37, 38, 53, 71, 179
Arensky, A., 3
Athens, 66
Auberjonois, René-Victor, 16, 21, 179
Auden, W. H., 40, 52, 53, 65, 71, 179
Australia, 62

Bach, J. S., 4, 68, 70, 130, 150
Bakst, Léon, 5, 7, 17, 26, 179
Balakirev, Mily, 3
Balanchine, George, 5, 31, 35, 43, 48, 51, 59, 62, 67, 71, 95, 107, 110, 148, 179
Ballets Russes, 5, 6, 24, 26, 33, 35, 36, 37, 39, 43
Balmont, Konstantin, 118, 179
Barcelona, 31
Bartók, Béla, 118
Beethoven, Ludwig van, 68, 70, 130
Belaiev, Mitrofan, 3, 4, 149
Benois, Alexandre, 5, 7, 9, 15, 35, 81, 179
Berg, Alban, 53; Three Orchestral Pieces, 73; Wozzeck, 87
Berlin, 39, 59, 68, 115

Berlin, Isaiah, 65, 180
Berners, Lord, 17, 180
Biarritz, 27, 31
Bolm, Adolph, 46, 180
Borodin, Alexander, 3; Prince Igor, 3
Boston, 37, 38, 56
Boulanger, Nadia, 46, 180
Boulez, Pierre, 54, 180
Brecht, Berthold, 83
Brussels, 38
Busoni, Ferrucio, 16
Byrd, William, 124

Carantec, 24
Casella, Alfredo, 102
Catania, 64
Chicago, 52, 63, 65, 67
Chopin, Frédéric, 6, 95, 103
Cimbalom, 77, 141
Cingria, Alexandre, 16
Cingria, Charles-Albert, 16, 71, 180
Clarens, 10, 14
Cocteau, Jean, 11, 13, 19, 31, 32, 33, 71, 86, 180
Coolidge, Elizabeth Sprague, 34
Couperin, François, 4
Craft, Robert, 53–4, 59, 61, 62, 66, 67, 68, 71, 129, 180
Cui, César, 3

Index

Dargomijsky, Alexander, 3, 27, 81, 149

de Bosset, Vera, *see under* Stravinsky

Debussy, Claude, 4, 8, 13, 25, 54, 81, 84, 115, 118–19; *Prélude à l'après-midi d'un Faune*, 10; *Pelléas et Mélisande*, 8

Delage, Maurice, 13

Delibes, Léo, 84

Diaghilev, Sergey, 5, 6, 7, 10, 12, 13, 14, 15, 17, 18, 22–3, 25, 26, 27, 28, 30, 31, 33, 35, 36, 37, 39, 42, 51, 67, 69, 71, 76, 79, 81, 102–3; *Liturgie*, 17

d'Indy, Vincent, 4

Dolin, Anton, 48, 181

Donaueschingen, 32, 112

Dukas, Paul, 4, 41

Dushkin, Samuel, 38, 39, 41, 71, 109, 181

Egypt, 63

Eliot, T. S., 6, 61, 65, 126, 181

Evenings of contemporary music (St Petersburg), 4, 56

'Evenings on the Roof' (Los Angeles), 56

Evian, 69

Falla, Manuel de, 13

'The Five', 3, 4, 5, 73, 149

Flonzaley String Quartet, 25, 181

Fokine, Mikhail, 5, 7, 9, 181

The Futurists, 17

Garches, 24

Geneva, 18, 23, 59

Genoa, 32

Gerhard, Roberto, *The Duenna*, 88

Gesualdo, Carlo, 130

Gide, André, 40–1, 86, 181

Glazunov, Alexander, 3, 5, 149

Glinka, Michael, 3, 26, 27, 81, 149; *A Life for the Tsar*, 3; *Russlan and Ludmilla*, 3

Graff, Robert, 61

Hamburg, 63, 64

Handel, G. F., 84

Harvard, 45

Hindemith, Paul, 39

Hollywood, 44, 46, 47, 57, 63, 66

Honegger, Arthur, 32

Horne, Marilyn, 68

Huxley, Aldous, 46, 52, 59, 64, 71, 182

Isherwood, Christopher, 71, 182

Israel, 63, 64

Janssen, Werner, 27

Jazz, 21–2, 77–8, 150

Jerusalem, 65

Josquin des Près, 150

Karsavina, Tamara, 9, 182

Kashperova, Mlle, 2

Kennedy, President J. F., 63, 64

Kholodovsky, Anna, *see under* Stravinsky

Kholodovsky, Kiril, 1

Khrennikov, Tikhon, 63, 182

Kireievsky, Peter, 16–17

Kirstein, Lincoln, 43, 51, 59, 182

Kochno, Boris, 26, 82, 182

Koussevitzky, Natalie, 38, 48, 99

Koussevitzky, Sergey, 9, 25, 31, 37, 38, 48, 182

Lausanne, 21, 23

Leibowitz, René, 54

Leningrad, *see* St Petersburg
Liadov, Anatol, 3, 7
Lifar, Sergey, 35, 183
Lisbon, 66
London, 12, 14, 15, 25, 36, 64
Los Angeles, 46, 47, 59, 68

Machaut, Guillaume de, 130
Madrid, 19, 25
Malmgreen, Eugene, 31n.
Mann, Thomas, 46, 183
Marinetti, Emilio, 17, 183
Marion, André, 53, 183
Markova, Alicia, 48, 183
Maryinsky Theatre (St Petersburg), 2, 3
Massine, Léonide, 5, 12, 17, 18, 23, 25, 79
Matisse, Henri, 23, 183
Messager, André, 15
Messiaen, Olivier, 54, 76n.
Milan, 33
Milhaud, Darius, 32, 183
Mitusov, Stepan, 3, 15, 70
Monday evening concerts (Los Angeles), 56, 65, 66
Monteux, Pierre, 11, 12, 15, 18, 37, 64, 100, 184
Monteverdi, Claudio, 34
Montreux, 59
Morges, 16
Morton, Lawrence, 56, 66, 184
Moscow, 15, 63
Mozart, W. A., 66, 105; *Così fan tutte*, 88; *Don Giovanni*, 88
Munich, 46, 59
Mussorgsky, Modeste, 3; *Boris Godunov*, 6, 81; *Khovansh-china*, 14, 174

Nabokov, Nicholas, 53, 68, 71, 184

Naples, 19
New York, 18, 43, 45, 50, 51, 59, 60, 63, 68
New Zealand, 63
Nice, 31
Nijinska, Bronislava, 5, 26, 27, 36, 184
Nijinsky, Vaslav, 7, 9, 10, 12, 18, 25, 71, 184
Nossenko, Catherine, *see under* Stravinsky
Nossenko, Gabriel, 2
Nossenko, Ludmilla, 2
Nossenko, Maria, 2

Oakland, 68
Oedipus Rex (Sophocles), 2, 32, 84
Onnou, Alphonse, 110, 184
Oranienbaum, 1
Organ, 51, 59, 121, 122
Oustilug, 2, 9, 10, 14, 16, 65

Palestrina, 124
Paris, 7, 9, 10, 12, 14, 18, 22, 24, 27, 30, 31, 36, 37, 39, 41, 46, 49, 54, 63, 66, 68, 81, 100, 115
Pearson, N. H., 53
Pergolesi, Giovanni, 23, 79, 150
Petrenko, Elizabeth, 4
Philippot, Michel, 54
Phoenix, 68
Picasso, Pablo, 5, 19, 23, 71, 79, 184–5
Pierné, Gabriel, 8, 18
Piston, Walter, 46
Poland, 1, 20, 65
Polignac, Princess Edmond de, 13, 18, 27, 28, 31, 32, 33, 40, 185
Pope Paul, 66
Poulenc, Francis, 105
Prévost, Germain, 110, 185

Index

Prokofiev, Sergey, 17; *The Buffoon*, 17; *Classical Symphony*, 88; *Second Piano Concerto*, 17

Pushkin, Alexander, 2, 26, 82, 114

Ramuz, Charles, 16, 20, 21, 25, 53, 71, 185

Ravel, Maurice, 4, 8, 13, 14, 27, 79, 115

Reinhart, Werner, 22, 23

Richter, Nicolas, 4

Rimsky-Korsakov, Andrei, 4

Rimsky-Korsakov, Nadezhda, 5

Rimsky-Korsakov, Nicolai, 2, 3, 4, 5, 15, 71, 114, 185; *Sadko*, 3; *Sheherazade*, 7, 36; *The Snow Maiden*, 18; *Soleil de minuit*, 18

Rimsky-Korsakov, Vladimir, 4, 63

Roerich, Nicholas, 5, 10, 12

Romanov, Boris, 15

Rome, 19, 31, 44, 59, 64, 69

Rose, Billy, 48

Rossini, Gioacchino, 86

Rubinstein, Anton, 2

Rubinstein, Artur, 9, 185

Rubinstein, Ida, 35, 36, 39, 43, 185

Sacher, Paul, 51, 62, 68, 185

St Petersburg, 1, 3, 4, 5, 6, 8, 9, 17, 26, 31, 36, 42, 56, 63, 73, 74, 81

Saint-Saëns, Camille, 84, 105

San Francisco, 68

Santa Fé, 64

Satie, Erik, 93, 102; *Parade*, 19

Scarlatti, Domenico, 19, 23

Schmitt, Florent, 11, 13, 41; *Tragédie de Salomé*, 11

Schoenberg, Arnold, 32, 46, 53, 55, 115, 118, 130, 149, 150–1; *Pierrot Lunaire*, 79, 115

Scriabin, Alexander, 3, 102, 118

Seattle, 67

Sergeyev, Nicolas, 26

Serov, Valentine, 3

Shilkret, Nathaniel, 48

Siloti, Alexander, 4, 6, 186

Snetkova, Mlle, 2

Sophocles, see under *Oedipus Rex*

Souvtchinsky, Pierre, 6, 45, 59, 67, 71, 186

Steegmuller, Francis, 66

Stockhausen, Karlheinz, 54

Stony Brook, 68

Stravinsky, Anna (*née* Kholodovsky, mother), 1

Stravinsky, Catherine (*née* Nossenko, 'Katia', first wife), 2, 3, 45, 53

Stravinsky, Feodor (father), 1, 3

Stravinsky, Goury (brother), 1, 2, 115

Stravinsky, Igor, classified works:-

CANTATAS, CHORAL WORKS

Anthem, 'the dove descending', 126, 138, 170

Ave Maria, 119, 170

Babel, 48, 120, 135, 170

Cantata, 52–3, 55, 118, 122, 170

Canticum Sacrum, 58–9, 60, 61, 89, 90, 122–3, 124, 136, 138, 170

Credo, 119, 170

Four Russian Peasant Songs ('*saucers*'), 16, 119, 170, 176

Introitus, 65, 126–7, 139, 170

Mass, 51, 60, 118, 120–2, 127, 133, 136, 170

Pater Noster, 71, 119, 170

Requiem Canticles, 66–7, 69, 127–129, 131, 139, 142, 170

A Sermon, a Narrative and a Prayer, 62, 89, 106, 125–6, 138, 144, 170

Symphony of Psalms, 37–8, 51, 58, 71, 88, 95, 119–20, 137, 143, 170

Threni, 60, 62, 65, 106, 124–5, 131, 133, 138 141, 144, 145, 152, 170

Zvezdoliki, 118, 170

DRAMATIC WORKS

Agon, 59, 78, 88–9, 90, 105, 138, 144, 169

Apollo, 34–5, 36, 38, 43, 49, 85, 95, 110, 151, 168

The Fairy's Kiss, 15, 35–6, 43, 85, 168, 175–6

The Firebird, 7, 18, 19, 22, 33, 62, 67, 72–3, 92, 101, 131, 134, 135, 142, 144, 168, 175

The Flood, 61–2, 64, 65, 88, 89–91, 138, 144, 145, 169

Histoire du soldat, 17, 19, 20–2, 28, 33, 36, 38, 67, 77–9, 80, 94, 103, 110, 130, 141, 142, 149–50, 152, 168, 175

Jeu de cartes, 43, 51, 86, 95, 135, 168

Mavra, 26, 27, 52, 81–2, 87, 149, 168, 175

Les Noces, 16, 17, 18, 19, 20, 28, 30, 65, 67, 79–80, 92, 117, 119, 132, 141, 142, 145, 147, 149–50, 168

Oedipus Rex, 2, 32–4, 38, 66, 83–84, 86, 134, 145, 168

Orpheus, 51, 59, 83, 86–7, 110, 132, 135, 168

Persephone, 40, 83, 85–6, 110, 132, 151, 168

Petrushka, 8, 11, 17, 19, 25, 27, 33, 38, 41, 50, 62, 73–4, 111, 142, 168, 175

Pulcinella, 23–4, 67, 79, 113, 143, 145, 168, 175

The Rake's Progress, 51–4, 55, 58, 81, 82, 87, 88, 152, 169, 176

Renard, 17, 18, 19, 20, 27, 77, 80, 141, 145, 168

Le Rossignol, 3, 7, 8, 15, 33, 35, 76, 81, 88, 145, 168, 175

Le Sacre du printemps, 8, 10–12, 14, 25, 27, 36, 47, 64, 68, 74–6, 80, 97, 130, 132, 134, 141, 151–2, 168

ORCHESTRAL WORKS

Capriccio, 37, 41, 86, 87, 105, 108, 109, 169

Circus Polka, 48, 99, 169

Concerto (piano and wind), 30–1, 37, 38, 104–5, 142–3, 169

Concerto (violin), 39, 109–10, 169

Concerto in D (strings), 51, 65, 87, 94, 100, 138, 169

Concerto in E flat ('Dumbarton Oaks'), 44, 94, 138, 169

Danses Concertantes, 48, 86, 94–95, 99, 132, 135, 169

Ebony Concerto, 100, 169

Fireworks, 5, 6, 21, 92, 169

Four Norwegian Moods, 47, 99, 169

Index

Greeting Prelude, 100, 169
Movements, 59, 60–1, 64, 89, 97, 101, 102, 105–7, 112, 131, 136–7, 138, 144, 152, 169
Ode, 47, 99, 169
Ragtime, 22, 103, 169
Scènes de Ballet, 48, 86, 99–100, 169
Scherzo à la Russe, 47, 99, 169
Scherzo Fantastique, 6, 92, 169
Symphonies of wind instruments, 25–6, 28, 92–3, 118, 169
Symphony in C, 44–6, 94–7, 137–138, 143, 147, 169
Symphony in E flat, 4, 5, 92, 169
Symphony in three movements, 50–1, 95, 97–9, 143, 147, 169
Variations for orchestra, 64, 65, 92, 101, 113, 133–4, 139, 144, 169

PIANO AND CHAMBER WORKS

Les cinq doigts, 25, 173, 177
Concertino, 38, 112, 173, 177
Concerto for two pianos, 41, 103–104, 108, 110, 173
Double canon, 60, 112, 138, 173
Duo Concertant, 39, 41, 110, 134, 139, 173
Elegy (viola), 110, 173
Epitaphium, 112, 126, 138, 152, 173
Étude for pianola, see under Study
Five easy pieces (piano duet), 19, 102, 173, 176
Four studies (piano), 102, 173
Octet, 28, 30, 56, 113, 142, 173
Piano-Rag-Music, 23, 103, 173
Septet, 56, 113–14, 173

Serenade (piano), 31–2, 103, 107–108, 173
Sonata (piano), 31, 103, 107
Sonata for two pianos, 102, 104, 173
Souvenir d'une Marche Boche, 173
Study for pianola ('Madrid'), 103, 111, 173, 176
Tango, 47, 103, 173, 177
Three easy pieces (piano duet), 102, 173, 176–7
Three pieces (clarinet), 22, 173
Three pieces (string quartet), 111, 173, 176

SONGS

Abraham and Isaac, 64, 65, 116-117, 138, 140–1, 172
Berceuse, 172
Berceuses du chat, 16, 77, 114, 116, 172
Elegy for J.F.K., 65, 116, 126, 128, 139, 172
The Faun and the Shepherdess, 2, 114, 171
Four Russian Songs, 115, 172, 177
In memoriam Dylan Thomas, 57, 112, 116, 172
The Owl and the Pussy-cat, 66, 116, 126, 139, 172
Pastorale, 5, 171, 176
Pribaoutki, 16, 77, 80, 114, 115, 171
Souvenirs de mon enfance, 14, 114, 171
Three Japanese Lyrics, 79, 115, 171
Three songs from William Shakespeare, 56, 115, 172

Tilimbom, see *Trois histoires*

Trois histoires pour enfants, 16, 56, 77, 119, 131, 172, 177

Two melodies (Gorodetzky), 4, 171

Two poems (Balmont), 56, 115, 171, 176

Two poems (Verlaine), 115, 119, 171, 176

TRANSCRIPTIONS, EARLY WORKS, BOOKS

Chant du Rossignol, 15, 23, 31, 175

Chronicles of my life, 12, 30, 42, 58, 61, 188

Eight Instrumental Miniatures, 93–4, 177

Four Studies for orchestra, 111, 176

Monumentum pro Gesualdo, 61, 174

Plaisanteries musicales, 4, 177

The Poetics of Music, 45, 188

Scherzo (piano), 102, 177

Sonata in F sharp minor (piano), 4, 177

Suites (small orchestra), 93, 176–177

Tres Cantiones Sacrae (Gesualdo), 61, 174

Vom Himmel hoch (Bach), 59, 174

Stravinsky, John (grandson), 192

Stravinsky, Ludmilla (daughter, 'Mika'), 14, 44, 102

Stravinsky, Maria Milena (daughter), 14, 45, 53

Stravinsky, Roman (brother), 1

Stravinsky, Soulima (son), 14, 41, 43, 53, 108, 192

Stravinsky, Theodore (son), 14, 53, 102, 192

Stravinsky, Vera (*née* de Bosset, second wife), 14, 30, 31n., 46, 63, 66, 67, 68, 69

Stravinsky, Youry (brother), 1

Survage, Léopold, 27

Tahiti, 63

Talachkino, 10

Tallis, Thomas, 124

Tansman, Alexander, 46, 53, 71, 97, 186

Tchaikovsky, Peter, 3, 26, 35, 85, 149; *Romeo and Juliet*, 114; *The Sleeping Beauty*, 3, 26, 100, 174

Tcherepnin, Nicolai, 3, 7; *Le Pavillon d'Armide*, 7

Tenichev, Princess, 10

Thomas, Dylan, 56–7, 61–2, 186

Tippett, Michael, *Concerto for Orchestra*, 97n.

Toronto, 67

Ussachevsky, Vladimir, 63

Venice, 32, 36, 52, 58, 59, 60, 61, 63, 66, 69, 122

Verdi, Giuseppe, 84; *Ballo in maschera*, 88; *Rigoletto*, 88

Voreppe, 39, 41

Wagner, Richard, 2, 80–1, 114, 146, 148, 151; *Lohengrin*, 3

Warsaw, 15, 16

Washington, 35, 44, 52

Weber, Margrit, 60

Webern, Anton, 53–5, 89, 115, 143, 147, 150, 151

Index

Weimar, 16
Welles, Orson, 47
Werfel, Franz, 46
Whiteman, Paul, 47, 187
Wiesbaden, 40

Wolf, Hugo, 68; *Spanisches Lieder-buch*, 175

Zürich, 16, 23, 68